EYES & SPIES

EYES & SPIES

HOW YOU'RE TRACKED AND WHY YOU SHOULD KNOW

Tanya Lloyd Kyi

Art by Belle Wuthrich

annick press
toronto + berkeley + vancouver

Edited by Linda Pruessen
Proofread by Stephanie Fysh
Designed by Belle Wuthrich

ANNICK PRESS LTD.

We acknowledge the support of the Canada Council for the Arts and the Ontario Arts Council, and the participation of the Government of Canada/la participation du gouvernement du Canada for our publishing activities.

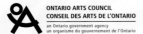 

CATALOGING IN PUBLICATION
Kyi, Tanya Lloyd, 1973-, author
        Eyes & spies : how you're tracked and why you should know / Tanya Lloyd Kyi ; art by Belle Wuthrich.

Includes bibliographical references and index.
Issued in print and electronic formats.
ISBN 978-1-55451-911-8 (hardback).—ISBN 978-1-55451-910-1 (paperback).—
ISBN 978-1-55451-912-5 (html).—ISBN 978-1-55451-913-2 (pdf)

        1. Data protection--Juvenile literature. 2. Privacy, Right of--Juvenile literature. I. Wuthrich, Belle, 1989-, illustrator II. Title. III. Title: Eyes and spies.

JC596.K94 2017   j323.44'8   C2016-906530-8
                                                        C2016-906531-6

Published in the U.S.A. by Annick Press (U.S.) Ltd.
Distributed in Canada by University of Toronto Press.
Distributed in the U.S.A. by Publishers Group West.

Printed in China

Visit us at: www.annickpress.com
Visit Tanya Lloyd Kyi at: tanyalloydkyi.com
Visit Belle Wuthrich at: bellewuthrich.com

Also available in e-book format.
Please visit www.annickpress.com/ebooks.html for more details. Or scan

CONTENTS

REC

INTRODUCTION	EYES AND SPIES	2
1	HALLWAY MONITORS	9
2	HOME SWEET HOME	27
3	STREET SENSE	44
4	CAUGHT IN THE WEB	59
5	SHOP 'TIL YOU DROP DATA	83
6	BIG BROTHER BOTHER	103
CONCLUSION	DRAWING THE LINE	122
	FURTHER READING	125
	SELECTED SOURCES	126
	INDEX	132
	ABOUT THE AUTHOR & ILLUSTRATOR	135

EYES AND SPIES

IMAGINE YOU'RE A SECRET AGENT assigned to track someone. How will you do it? Hide in a doorway across the street from his house and wait for him to emerge? Then you can shadow him as he walks to school, or work, or a friend's place. You might even slip into a restaurant booth near where he's eating and eavesdrop on his conversations.

Maybe ... if you're pretending to be in a classic detective movie. In real life—21st-century life—there's no need for all that sneaking around. The person you're tracking is probably carrying a smartphone, so his phone manufacturer, his Internet provider, and a few app designers all know where he is, every moment of every day. As a government operative, you can request those records directly from the companies.

And snooping around in a restaurant is plain silly. Why not monitor his emails instead? You can use security cameras to track his movements, and scanners to watch his car. Scroll through his tweets to see who's meeting him, or where he's heading.

You can probably find his address, phone number, and photo online, plus a list of his Instagram followers and maybe even some

invitations to local events. You might read about him in a school newspaper article or in a list of sports results. It won't be hard to paint a picture of his daily life.

The ability to easily gather all that information about someone seems a little creepy. But you're a secret agent on official government business. You'll only be searching the Internet for the names of terrorists and criminals. Right?

Not necessarily.

Because computers can collect billions of items of information about every single one of us and scan that information for patterns, we're all being "watched." Yes, governments track us so they can pinpoint terrorism suspects. But lots of other people and organizations are also trying to find out who we are and what we do. Corporations analyze our preferences and habits so they can tailor their advertising. Police forces monitor our movements so they can target crime more effectively. In many cases, we're even tracking ourselves then releasing our data to the world.

Some people think that's fine. After all, there are huge benefits to sharing things over the Internet. We meet new friends through social media, spread information, and exchange viewpoints. We market our music or art. By listing our location, we learn about nearby stores or events. It's often fun to share things freely and make our thoughts and ideas public.

THE CREEPY LINE

IN 2010, ERIC SCHMIDT, the CEO of Google, said that his company's policy was to "get right up to the creepy line and not cross it." For example, you might feel okay about the company keeping track of your Google searches. But what if a Google employee turned up at your door with McDonald's coupons after you searched "hamburgers"? That would seem invasive.

This whole idea raises some questions:

→ Where exactly is the "creepy line"?

→ Would everyone draw it in the same place?

→ Who should decide?

The Creepy Line sections throughout this book will ask you to consider where you might set the boundaries, if you ruled the world.

Besides, many people believe that surveillance makes everyone safer.

Is that true?

If someone decided to stand on his bed, use his hairbrush as a microphone, and lip-synch to the latest episode of *The Voice,* would he want people peeking at him through his laptop's webcam? Probably not! What if a girl texted a friend about her most recent crush? Would she want other people reading that message?

Or what about this ...

Imagine you're shopping in a posh department store, and you take a selfie posing in a fur coat made from endangered zebralope pelts. You send it to your frenemy, who puts the photo online. Okay, that's silly, but it's not world-ending. Unless ... 10 or 20 years from now,

you decide you'd like to be Minister for the Environment. Or head of the Society for the Prevention of Cruelty to Animals. Then the media finds your old photo on the Internet and reposts it for all to see!

SMILE—YOU'RE ON CAMERA!

THE WAY WE ACT when we know we're being watched is different from the way we act when we're alone. Scientists say that when people are in groups or under surveillance, we tend to conform. We're more careful, and more likely to act the way everyone else does. We don't necessarily experiment with new ideas.

Way back in 1791, Jeremy Bentham designed what he thought would be the ideal prison. He called it the panopticon. It was a circular structure built around a central core. The prisoners' cells lined the outer ring. From the center, the guards could see any prisoner at any time.

Jeremy suggested that, because the prisoners had no way of knowing when they were being monitored, they would have to behave at all times as if the guards were watching. They would then self-reform into model citizens.

Jeremy's prison was never built, but some privacy activists say we now live in a "digital panopticon." As we shop online or post on social media, we know that others are tracking and judging our lives. That "I'm being watched" feeling can affect the way we live and think. We might start to pick and choose what we post in order to project a certain image of ourselves. We might behave more carefully and try to blend in better with our friends. Some people worry that when we know we're being observed, it can change the events we choose to attend, the causes we champion, or the politicians we support. Imagine you see this story in the news: "Government Spy Caught Posing as Member of Local Environmental Group." You might think twice about joining that group, even if you believe in their campaigns.

The following pages delve into the ways we're monitored, from the number of footsteps we take each day, to the fast-food companies we "like" on Facebook, to the things we flush down the toilet. Each chapter asks three simple questions:

1. WHO'S WATCHING, AND WHY?

2. WHERE IS THE LINE BETWEEN PUBLIC AND PRIVATE?

3. HOW CAN YOU KEEP YOUR SECRETS TO YOURSELF?

HALLWAY MONITORS

SINCE 2004, many parents in Japan have received email messages whenever their kids arrive at or depart from school. How? The kids carry radio frequency identification (RFID) tags in their schoolbags. These tiny tags communicate with "readers" up to 10 meters (30 feet) away. The systems automatically take attendance, then send the information to teachers and parents. In some parts of the country, schools are even experimenting with RFID systems that track students as they travel through nearby neighborhoods.

In Japan, most kids have traditionally walked themselves to class and back.

The World Health Organization says: Fantastic! Japan has some of the healthiest kids in the world.

But parents said: *Dôshiyô!* What if our kids are robbed or kidnapped while they're alone on the streets? Though Japan has a very low crime rate, parents still worried. By installing RFID systems, schools have made many families feel more secure.

They've also started a trend for the rest of the world to follow.

THE FAST TRACK

RADIO FREQUENCY identification wasn't designed to track kids. It was originally used by World War II forces to help sort friendly planes from enemy bombers. Decades later, scientists figured out how to embed extra information inside RFID tags. Two-way radios called "readers" could bounce energy off the tags and decode the results.

In the 1990s, researchers made miniature versions. Suddenly, RFID tags could be placed everywhere. The devices tracked shipments at ports, kept passports secure, and allowed employees to open security doors. They were attached to products as small as individual lipstick tubes. They allowed companies to track their shipments from factory floors right into the stores, making inventory much, much easier.

Today, stores such as Walmart require suppliers to attach RFID chips to all products. Libraries use tags to track their books. Veterinarians attach them to pets so the animals won't get lost. And biologists clip them to wildlife for research purposes.

But kids aren't the same as lipstick tubes, library books, or puppies.

NO BLEEPING WAY

IN JANUARY 2013, Andrea Hernandez was suspended from John Jay High in San Antonio, Texas. The school had implemented an RFID tracking system. Each student received an ID card embedded with a tag. That way, the school could tell how many students were on campus.

John Jay High already had 200 security cameras. So the chips weren't necessarily meant to keep students safe. They were intended to increase attendance. The school received funding based on how many kids were present each morning. But any kid who was taking a bathroom break or getting a form signed at the office, wasn't necessarily counted. With RFID tags, the school could count more accurately and—hopefully—gain more money. The tags could also be used to allow students to buy cafeteria items, access library books, and get special-event tickets.

But Andrea said she didn't like being tracked. She was a devout Catholic, and claimed a passage from the Bible forbade her from wearing such a tag. When she was suspended for refusing to wear her ID, she sued the school district.

Civil liberties associations, privacy advocates, and even a famous hacker group called Anonymous all sprang to Andrea's defense.

Andrea's school said: Don't jump to conclusions.

The principal decided that because of her privacy and religious concerns, Andrea could wear the school's ID card without the RFID. She could still participate in all school activities, tag or no tag.

But Andrea believed that wearing *any* ID card was prohibited by the Bible. She also said that if she wore a card, it would make it seem as if she supported the school's program.

A judge ruled against her. According to the court, the school's offer was fair, and Andrea had no case.

Andrea switched schools, and only returned to John Jay High once the RFID program was dismantled. (It turned out that the tags hadn't increased attendance anyway!)

Some preschools in Europe, Asia, and North America now offer live video streaming. Parents can log on from their computers and check on their children in real time.

SMILE! YOU'RE ON CAMERA

JOHN JAY HIGH wasn't the first school—and it likely won't be the last—to spark controversy by asking students to carry trackers, or attach them to bags or clothing. Over the past few decades, security cameras have popped up in hallways and cafeterias from California to Copenhagen. They're in half of all American schools and in more than 100,000 across Britain. Even cameras inside classrooms are growing steadily more common around the world.

There's not much research to prove whether or not cameras make schools safe. Still, a poll by Ipsos Public Affairs in 2013 found that over half of parents across North America preferred schools equipped with surveillance cameras.

Ipsos didn't ask students how they felt about the filming.

THE CREEPY LINE

KENYA'S LIMURU MODEL PRIMARY SCHOOL had a major problem. Thieves had been targeting schools in the city, knowing the buildings were an easy source of books and computer equipment. At other schools, six guards had been killed during break-ins.

The elementary school responded by installing alarms and security cameras everywhere. Suddenly, teachers were working harder (knowing they were on camera), parents felt more comfortable sending their kids to school, and enrollment went up.

But students were constantly under watch. Any classroom projects, gossip with friends, or illicit snack-food runs were caught on film. Some people worried the cameras would teach students that constant monitoring was normal. Or that when class discussions were recorded, students might not freely express their ideas.

WHAT DO YOU THINK? In especially dangerous areas, is it worth sacrificing student freedom and privacy for the sake of safety? If you were a student in Limuru, Kenya, would you choose a school with or without security cameras?

CHEATERS BEWARE

FOR TWO GRUELING DAYS, students sweat over their desks. Question after question about Chinese, math, English, and several optional subjects. At stake: future schooling, careers, destinies.

Every year, up to 10 million Chinese students take the National College Entrance Exam. Those who succeed can look forward to university classes. Those who fail might find themselves working factory jobs. The pressure is so intense, there are often dozens of suicide attempts in the weeks before the exam.

To prepare for testing, some students cram. Others cheat. In the month before the 2015 tests, authorities in the city of Louyang arrested 23 people. Some had hired people to impersonate them, equipping the imposters with fake fingerprints on plastic membranes; others had shopped for radio-equipped pens or glasses with transmitters attached. The students who were caught were banned from the exam for three years.

The Louyang organizers then unveiled one more anti-cheating plan: a drone. As the exam got underway, organizers launched a six-armed flying robot, equipped with scanners to detect radio transmission signals. The drone could hover about 500 meters (1,650 feet) above the test site.

No signals were detected during the 2015 exam—perhaps because the officials had gone to such lengths to publicize their anti-cheating campaign.

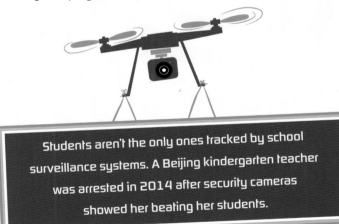

Students aren't the only ones tracked by school surveillance systems. A Beijing kindergarten teacher was arrested in 2014 after security cameras showed her beating her students.

TEACHER

STUDENT

WEBCAM WATCH

SURVEILLANCE CAMERAS ARE USUALLY easy to spot, but what about teachers who monitor their students through more hidden means—perhaps through the cameras built into laptops and tablets? Or through software that tracks student activities?

Plenty of teachers design lessons for use with laptop computers and tablets. Many colleges offer online courses. And there are benefits to watching the way people behave on their computers. For example, if students rewind the same portion of a video over and over again, their teacher can tell they're having trouble understanding it. Technology is also helping students write exams from remote locations. A soldier serving overseas, for example, might be able to write an exam on a laptop while a supervisor halfway around the world watches through the webcam.

But like any tool, laptop and tablet surveillance can be used well or poorly. And several schools have found themselves in high-tech hot water after secretly spying on students.

In 2010, a school district in Pennsylvania gave out more than 2,000 fancy new laptops to students to use at school or at home. Score! Except that each laptop had a webcam that could be turned on remotely by a school administrator.

Fifteen-year-old Blake Robbins found out about his webcam the hard way. He was hauled in front of his vice-principal and accused of taking drugs while at home, in his bedroom. (He said those "drugs" were actually candy.) After seeing the evidence—shots taken from his own laptop—he sued his school district. He said the webcam-watching was an invasion of his privacy.

The school claimed it hadn't meant to track Blake at home. Laptop software designed to prevent theft had kicked in automatically and clicked the photos. But that didn't really explain why the school had saved 56,000 images plucked from the webcams of various students.

After the case made major media waves, the school district chose to settle out of court. It coughed up $175,000 for Blake and another $425,000 for Blake's lawyer.

Hackers also spy through webcams. That's why computer experts suggest we keep our virus scanners up to date. Some people even put sticky notes over their webcams ... just in case.

B IS FOR BIOMETRY

IRIS SCAN COMPLETE. ACCESS GRANTED.

Biometrics is usually about checking to see if people really are who they say they are. Just like in spy movies, iris scans, hand scans, or fingerprints can be used to confirm identity. Machines can even detect differences in individuals' postures, voices, or scents. Fingerprints and iris scans are sometimes used at border crossings to increase security. And fingerprints and DNA databases are used to track criminals. There are even researchers working on ways to use biometrics to prevent auto theft—a sensor in the seat could detect the car owner's posture. If someone with different posture tried to drive, the ignition could turn itself off.

So what does this have to do with school? Well, imagine that your cafeteria lunch special today is spaghetti. If you'd like garlic toast with that, no problem. Just swipe your fingerprint, and the extra charge will be automatically added to your account. Each fingerprint, palm, or retina scanner converts students into data, and then stores the data.

Governments in different countries have arrived at drastically different viewpoints on whether or not it's okay to track student biometrics. The Hong Kong privacy commissioner put a stop to school fingerprint scans in 2006. That same year, a preschool in Britain made the news when it finger-printed three-year-olds to make sure they returned their library books.

Fingerprint and hand scans are most common in schools in Britain and the United States, and they've caused plenty of controversy in both places.

One concern is that more and more schools are collecting data, then storing that data on serv-ers connected to the Internet. Students' personal information could be stolen by hackers, or it could be shared with governments and corporations. (For more about why corporations might want that data, see chapter 5.)

SECURITY SAYS:
Safe, easy, and effective. What's the big deal?

PRIVACY SAYS:
Those records could stick around forever. We need new privacy laws … faster than you can say "Place your thumb here."

THE CREEPY LINE

TORONTO PRINCIPAL RON FELSEN was sick of students puking on the dance floor. He'd had to cancel a Halloween dance after only an hour because so many dancers were falling down drunk. None of Ron's anti-drinking efforts had worked. Frustrated, he met with parents and came up with a plan: everyone attending the 2014 prom would need to pass a Breathalyzer test.

Student council representatives didn't like this idea, however. They contacted the Canadian Civil Liberties Association, which helped them take their school to court. Breathalyzer plans were put on hold as the case proceeded. And in 2015, the Supreme Court decided that mandatory breath tests infringed on student rights.

WHAT DO YOU THINK? If drinking is out of control at school dances, should students agree to a breath test at the door? **?**

THE PRIVACY PUZZLE

OPPONENTS OF RFID CHIPS, classroom cameras, and biometrics point to one major concern: privacy. There's a concept called *in loco parentis*. In Latin legal-speak, it means that teachers and administrators are official guardians while kids are in school, so they're allowed to act like parents. They can confiscate cellphones, for example, or order students to empty their pockets.

But being watched by teachers is not the same as living under the constant eye of video surveillance. According to privacy advocates, it's different in five key ways:

1. **CAMERAS AND CHIPS** aren't kid stuff. Legally, minors can't agree to surveillance the same way adults can. Plus, attendance at school is kind of required. Kids can't choose to avoid the cameras.

2. **PEOPLE CHANGE.** As you go through school, you experiment with different personality traits and behaviors. If you feel like you're always watched, you might not explore the weird and wild aspects of your inner self. Like a prisoner in a panopticon, you might work harder to blend in.

3. **SELF-CONTROL 101.** If you're acting properly because a camera's watching or because an RFID tag is tracking you, could that prevent you from forming your own ideas about which behaviors are okay and which are not?

4. **THE PRESSURE!** Imagine your parents watching you 24 hours a day. Sometimes you need your own space.

5. **FINGER-POINTING.** Cameras aren't about safety; they're about judgment. A camera can't protect you from getting beat up. It simply helps identify who's at fault.

PRIVACY SAYS:

Many privacy experts believe that, at the very least, students should have a say in whether or not their classrooms incorporate cameras. That's because schools are creating future citizens. Teachers should be encouraging students to discuss choices and ethics.

It's also important for kids to know their rights. In most places, students have the right to remain silent when questioned by school staff. But rules about personal privacy vary from region to region.

HERE ARE SOME SUGGESTIONS:

→ **LOOK UP** the rules about surveillance cameras in your city or country. You can often find these online, sometimes through a civil liberties website.

→ **FIND OUT** about your school's policy on surveillance cameras. Suggest that the rules be posted.

→ **LAUNCH** a class project or a debate to explore the boundaries between privacy and school security.

CLASS DISMISSED

SO PARENTS AND TEACHERS want to keep kids safe. But some students don't want to be monitored, and many experts say that surveillance is bad for free speech and education.

Two researchers in Japan have a suggestion. Japan, after all, is a leader in student surveillance. So Arisa Ema and Yuko Fujigaki presented parents with a selection of scenarios, asking which would help them feel more secure:

→ Would it help if they could contact their kids through the RFID tags?

→ What if there were networked RFID readers throughout neighborhoods?

→ Should RFID tags be implanted under kids' skin?

Arisa and Yuko also took a look at parents' beliefs, home lives, and relationships. Here's what they discovered: most things made no difference to anxiety levels. Parents didn't worry any less if their kids were driven to school, or if kids had their own phones. It didn't matter if there were relatives living nearby. There wasn't even a difference between the security concerns of parents whose children had never faced danger and those of parents whose kids had been in accidents.

In the end, Arisa and Yuko found only one significant variable: the parents who felt they'd done a good job of raising their kids—those

who had "confidence in nurturing"—didn't feel such a strong need to have their kids tracked.

The Japanese study suggests that one simple step might help people feel better about security: parents and kids should talk more often.

>ACTION ALERT< Talk to your parents. Show them you understand the dangers of the world and know how to deal with them.

HOME SWEET HOME

IN 1926, George Thomas was eight years old. He was allowed to walk anywhere he wanted. Often, he'd walk 10 kilometers (6 miles) to his favorite fishing spot. By himself.

Jack Hattersley turned eight in 1950, in the same area of Sheffield, England. Jack was allowed to walk 1.6 kilometers (1 mile) to play in a wooded area. He also walked to school on his own, and to the homes of his friends. Jack grew up to become George's son-in-law.

Jack's daughter (and George's granddaughter) was named Vicki. She turned eight in 1979. She was still allowed to do a lot of things independently—though not quite so far from home. She could ride her bike to friends' houses or to the local swimming pool.

In 2007, Vicki's son Edward (great-grandson of George Thomas and grandson of Jack) turned eight. By himself, he was only allowed to walk to the end of his street.

So how did kids of the same family, in the space of four generations, go from far-flung freedom to supreme supervision? That was the question first asked by English researcher Dr. William Bird in 2007, as part of an ongoing project called Natural England.

The answers were complicated. The kids themselves were happy to stay inside, playing video games or watching TV. Their parents

worried about traffic and kidnapping. But Dr. Bird argues that keeping kids close to home might be hurting them more than helping. Many researchers believe that time spent in nature—the way George Thomas whiled away his hours at a fishing hole, or Jack Hattersley played in the woods—helps kids better handle worries and stress. So kids who play inside instead of roaming might actually be at greater risk of things like anxiety or depression.

SECURITY SAYS:
The world's getting more and more scary. We need to keep tabs on our kids.

BUNDLES OF JOY

SOME EXPERTS SAY that parents have grown more protective because, over the years, views on youth have changed. Society has started to see kids as needing constant protection.

Imagine this scene: new parents curl up on the couch, watching their little bundle of joy on a baby monitor. The market for baby monitors continues to grow, and few people argue with their usefulness. Parents want to know when their babies cry. Plus, babies

PRIVACY SAYS:
In North America, violent crime rates are lower today than they were in the 1970s.

don't need much privacy, and they *do* demand fairly constant care. So what's the problem with baby monitors?

Well, privacy advocates have a few concerns:

1. **PARENTS IN PANIC MODE.** Attentiveness is a good thing. But do parents need to see their infants with infrared night vision or listen to ambient sounds with a high-quality, static-dampening microphone? Should they cough up the cash for machines that measure nursery temperatures, or wearable devices that track a baby's sleep patterns? And could parents become more focused on their baby monitoring apps than on their actual baby?

2. **THE LONG LENS.** Parenting anxieties don't necessarily disappear as kids grow older. Some parents move from baby monitors to nanny cams—miniature cameras that can be placed inside stuffed animals, tucked behind clocks, or hidden above picture frames. Nanny cams allow parents to peek at their kids any time they like, watch how a babysitter disciplines or answers questions, or check whether everyone's eating a delicious lunch. But if kids (and nannies!) don't realize they're being filmed, nanny cams can be invasive.

3. HACK ATTACK. Many baby monitors and nanny cams transmit images to phones or laptops via the Internet. Unfortunately, anything connected to the Internet can be hacked. Some parents have even heard unfriendly voices coming from their monitors.

Maybe baby monitors have gone a little extreme, and we should probably be very careful when connecting cameras to the Internet. Still, everyone agrees that babies *do* need watching.

What about when kids are 7? Or 17?

YOU ARE HERE

THERE ARE FOUR Global Positioning System satellites in the sky above you, right now, no matter where on Earth you are.

The Global Positioning System, or GPS, was developed by the American military in the 1970s to help them calculate exact coordinates. They were carrying missiles on moving ships and needed to be sure they could aim precisely at targets.

The government knew GPS could be useful to shipping and trucking companies, search-and-rescue organizations, and individual drivers and hikers. But they were worried other military forces might use the technology, too. So when the United States first shared GPS with the public in the 1980s, it was only in a less reliable, scrambled form.

Then, in 2000, the Americans decided the public benefits of GPS outweighed any security concerns. They removed the final barriers and allowed people and companies to access accurate signals. Suddenly, cars, avalanche beacons, cellphones—even dog collars—could use technology to pinpoint an exact location.

A GPS receiver reads high-frequency, low-power radio signals from at least three satellites. It then calculates the time those signals took to travel—a process called "trilateration."

It takes 24 satellites to provide GPS coverage around the world, and the United States has a few backups floating up there, too. So whether you're standing on an Arctic ice floe or the peak of Everest, you can figure out where you are.

And so can your parents.

WHERE'S WALDO NOW?

IT'S THE SIZE OF A DECK OF CARDS and can be zipped into a child's backpack. Or it's brightly colored and snaps onto a child's wrist. Or it's a waterproof band that costs only five dollars and lasts a year.

GPS tracking devices for children come in all shapes and sizes. Some are designed for very young children, with only one call-home button. Others look like high-tech watches. All of them allow parents to pop open their laptops or check their phones and—*voilà!*—see their child's location. Some devices will notify parents if a child leaves preset "safe zones." Some will even measure how fast the child is traveling. Once kids are old enough to carry their own phones,

As kids geared up for Christmas in 2014, protesters denounced a toy called Elf on the Shelf. The figurine was meant to sit in a different location each day. Parents could say, "Be good, kiddo. That elf is helping Santa make his 'naughty' and 'nice' lists." It was a simple toy that didn't actually "watch" anyone at all, but opponents suggested it was training kids to accept a life of constant surveillance.

trackers are unnecessary. A smartphone offers all the surveillance a protective parent could want. Like GPS trackers, phone apps can be used to set travel boundaries. Some apps even alert parents when their kids enter the house. Many alarm companies offer a similar service. When parents are out of the house, they can receive a signal every time the front door opens, and even see, via video feed, who's coming and going. So if that big group of gamers is visiting again and there isn't any homework getting done, Mom or Dad can take immediate action.

TOY TROUBLE

AROUND THE WORLD, there are toy boxes and shelves filled with tech devices designed specifically for kids. But just like baby monitors, connected toys can be hacked. In November 2015, some security experts warned parents not to buy a Wi-Fi-enabled Barbie, suggesting the doll was easy to access remotely and the toy microphone could be used as a listening device.

A month later, the toy tech company VTech announced a hacker had stolen the private information of 4.8 million customers. Someone had gained access to children's names and home addresses.

It seemed that VTech hadn't properly protected its customer records. But many said parents were partly to blame. Thousands had bought connected devices and created online accounts, blindly putting their trust in a company known for toys, not cybersecurity.

THE CREEPY LINE

AMERICAN FAMILY INSURANCE offers a free program to the families of novice drivers. A tiny camera records only when it detects a driver slamming on the brakes, taking corners too fast, or putting the pedal to the metal.

The Teen Safe Driver program says that once families install the camera, seatbelt use goes from 54 to 100 percent, and the most unpredictable drivers improve by 70 percent. Parents say they feel more relaxed with the cameras installed. So, what do teens think?

Some say the cameras are a blatant attack on their privacy. Others say the cameras are worthwhile, because once parents feel more comfortable with how their kids are driving, they're willing to offer more freedom.

DIGITAL DILEMMAS

ONE RESEARCH FIRM ESTIMATES
that 70 million people are tracking their family members in North America and Europe alone. So, is it a terrible thing to watch over your kids? Here are a two reasons people say trackers are tops:

1. Knowing where their kids are makes parents feel more relaxed, which gives kids the time and freedom to roam with their friends.

2. A cellphone app can automatically shut down the phone when the device is moving quickly—one way to prevent texting while driving, which causes 11 teen deaths each day in the United States alone. Kids with autism are sometimes prone to wandering and getting lost, so a tracker can be a lifesaver ... literally.

GPS trackers might also help alleviate the number one fear of many parents: kidnapping. Between 2006 and 2011, kidnapping rates in Mexico more than tripled. In 2015, the U.S. government issued a warning to travelers planning to visit Mexico, saying that more than 100,000 people had been kidnapped there in 2012, and only 1,317

of these cases had been reported to the police.

Brazil faces similar problems; while only a few hundred kidnappings make the official police record, residents believe

In China, shoes implanted with tracking devices were developed for senior citizens with dementia. In 2015, a company called 361 Degrees produced four brightly colored styles for kids.

thousands more occur each year. Some victims are criminals themselves, involved in the drug trade. Others are innocent, targeted by people who hope to make quick cash through ransom payments. Still others are victims of political corruption.

Because there are so few kidnapping statistics, it's impossible to know how many victims are young people. Still, families in both Mexico and Brazil have invested in GPS and RFID trackers, hoping to safeguard their children.

But some experts accuse companies of exaggerating GPS effectiveness and preying on parents' fears. A device with a signal strong enough to allow police to track a victim for hours or days would need a battery. That means it would be big enough for kidnappers to easily find and destroy.

SUPER SPIES

TECHNOLOGY ALLOWS some parents to get super-sneaky.

→ With keytracking programs, parents can monitor every click and read every email—without telling their kids.

→ For moms and dads who worry when their teens hit the road, there are GPS devices that attach under the car dashboard. If they want, parents can even use microphone-equipped versions to listen to in-car conversations.

→ With a kit, parents can look for traces of drugs by swiping the surface of something a teen often touches—a bedroom doorknob, for example, or a cellphone. Add a drop or two of a chemical mix, and it's possible to check for the presence of more than 20 illegal drugs.

When surveyed, most parents say they trust their kids and would never use this sort of test or device. Research has shown that upper-class parents feel especially confident they know what their kids are up to. They're even less likely to resort to spyware.

But regardless of income or class, most moms and dads change their answers in certain circumstances. For example, what if their teen was suddenly staying out late, flunking math, and not sleeping properly? Then, parents say, peeking at emails, testing doorknobs, or recording conversations would become a lot more tempting.

THE CREEPY LINE

MARTHA AND MATTHEW FOSTER live with their kids in a New York City building with big windows that face the street. Anyone can see inside.

In 2013, a photographer named Arne Svenson zoomed his telephoto lens and took pictures of the family, then displayed the images as part of a show called "The Neighbors."

The Fosters said the photographer invaded their privacy. They sued. But a judge said if they chose to live in a glass box, then other people could choose to peek inside.

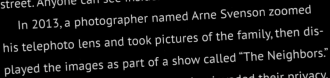

WHAT DO YOU THINK? Does a curtain of privacy require an actual curtain?

ACTION ALERT

How can teens negotiate with their parents about technology when parents are the ones setting the rules, but teens are the ones with a better understanding of the tools? American researchers interviewed more than 200 parents and kids over a period of seven years to identify strategies that worked for both sides. If your family disagrees about cellphones or Internet use, here are some options to consider:

→ **AGREE TO USE** software that will block certain sites.

→ **IF YOUR PARENTS** don't thoroughly understand how a piece of technology works, recruit trusted family members or friends to help explain it.

→ **PLACE YOUR COMPUTER** in a common room, where your parents can walk by while you're online.

→ **OFFER TO PAY** part of the cost for cellphone fees or Internet access.

Most of these strategies boil down to the same thing: the more trust that exists between parents and kids, and the more communication, the easier things become.

TrUST Me

LET'S ASSUME that you're not engaged in questionable behavior and you're not likely to be kidnapped anytime soon. Do you still need a GPS tracker?

There are lots of parenting gurus who say, "No, no way, never—children should not be tracked." They believe that part of childhood and adolescence involves exploring the limits of independence. When you're 8, maybe you're allowed to play in the park across the street by yourself. At 12, you're allowed as far as the corner store. When you're 15, you ride the city bus to school, you take yourself to soccer practice, and you spend Saturday afternoons at the beach with your friends. Each stage involves new levels of trust.

1. Alone at the park? Your parents obviously *trust* you'll act responsibly.

2. Walking on your own? You decide not to hitchhike, because you don't necessarily *trust* the passing strangers.

3. Hanging at the beach with your friends? You keep their secrets and they watch your back—you've built your friendships based on *trust*.

Trust comes in many forms, and we need all those variations by the time we reach adulthood. We need to rely on our own rules of behavior, believe in our own abilities, develop close relationships with our friends, and choose whether or not to welcome new people into our lives.

Can you develop all these skills if your parents are always watching?

Research shows that as people are trusted with more responsibility, they actually become more trustworthy.

THE ART OF GETTING LOST

MEET A COLLECTION of smart and sneaky kids.

In 2014, researchers staked out a housing complex in Ireland to see how kids and moms used cellphones. For moms, phones were a way to keep watch over their children from a distance. When their kids were playing a few blocks away, moms felt they still had control.

But kids saw their phones as symbols of independence, and many found their own ways to limit parental control—whether by

texting instead of answering calls, claiming they had a dead cell battery, or "forgetting" the cell was on silent mode.

And cellphones can work both ways in discussions about time and place. A mom can call and order her daughter home. But just as easily, a daughter can call and negotiate one more hour away.

Back in 1926, George Thomas said goodbye to his mother and walked to his fishing hole 10 kilometers (6 miles) from home. From the time he left the front door until the time he returned, she had to trust him. She had no other choice—cellphones weren't invented until 1973, and wouldn't be practical for most people to use until two decades later! Today, parents have many more tracking options. But as those kids in the Irish housing development showed, tracking's not perfect, and kids often find their own ways to explore.

STREET SENSE

PREPARE TO SAY "CHEESE." Then say it again, and again, and again ... In the past decade, the number of cameras in public spaces has exploded. It's difficult to figure out exactly how many there are, because they're installed by all sorts of people and organizations: police forces, businesses, banks, news agencies, and ordinary homeowners.

→ A 2013 study counted 5.9 million security cameras in Britain.

→ In the United States, more than 30 million cameras shoot 4 billion hours of video each week.

→ Journalists in Hong Kong calculated 50,000 cameras in the city.

Experts estimate that there are between 210 and 245 million active security cameras around the world. That's a lot of footage! As the cameras roll, more and more people are wondering: How do all those lenses affect the way we live?

TO CATCH A CRIMINAL

ON APRIL 15, 2013, spectators packed the streets of Boston, cheering as sweat-drenched runners approached the finish line of the city's annual marathon. Then a blast rocked the area. Twelve seconds later, another explosion. Bits of metal tore through the air. Runners and fans collapsed, people screamed, and sirens blared.

Three people were killed, including an eight-year-old boy. Another 180 were injured, some of them losing arms or legs.

Police and military investigators swooped in. After finding the remains of two homemade bombs, they set to work identifying suspects. They went from store to store along the street, collecting surveillance video. Then the head of the local Federal Bureau of Investigation (FBI) office made a public announcement asking people to share their smartphone photos and videos. Together, those sources gave the investigators one million hours of video footage.

The Boston bombing investigation almost went awry when a newspaper posted a photo of "suspects" who turned out to be bystanders. The FBI released its own photos quickly after to make sure no other innocent people were targeted by the media.

Experts watched clip after clip, and computers analyzed the videos, too. Specialized software allowed the FBI to search for unusual patterns, such as cars that turned up repeatedly in different places.

By April 18, investigators had two suspects: Dzhokhar and Tamerlan Tsarnaev. While attempting to escape later that day, the brothers stole a car and shot at police, killing one officer. Tamerlan was wounded in the shoot-out, then run over by his own brother. Dzhokhar was captured the next day, after a massive manhunt.

SIDE BENEFITS

IN BOSTON, cameras allowed police to track and capture two terrorists in record time. Security cameras are useful for more ordinary things as well:

→ They can track the flow of people inside train stations and help architects design better pathways.

→ They can show store managers whether their signs are properly directing shoppers.

→ They can detect traffic accidents and help direct commuters.

But privacy activists say cameras—even useful ones—have serious side effects. Here are just few:

→ They can be used to spy on people who are making perfectly legal "trouble." For example, they might be used to keep an eye on environmental activists or other legitimate protesters.

→ Camera operators can be biased. If the person behind a camera thinks criminals are all black people, or young men, or short people with pink hair, then that camera can be focused unjustly.

→ They can be used to create safe places for certain people, and less safe areas for others.

security says:
Surveillance made the soccer tournament safe for visitors and the city safer for residents.

privacy says:
Surveillance made the city safer for *some* people. Thousands of others were treated as if they were dangerous, unsightly, or less worthy of safety.

In 2010, Johannesburg, South Africa, hosted the FIFA World Cup. Four years later, researchers revisited the city. They found that during the event, high-crime areas around the soccer stadiums were safer than usual, probably because of extra police patrols and security cameras equipped with facial recognition software and linked to crime databases.

The World Cup was a big success, with no major security incidents. But all that extra surveillance meant that homeless people in those zones were forced from their neighborhoods. Street vendors were arrested and illegal immigrants targeted. And many of the cameras put in place for the World Cup stayed in place when the event was over. Some of the displaced people never managed to return.

PERSONAL SPACE ... IN PUBLIC

HAVE YOU PAID YOUR MORTGAGE LATELY?
Talked to your landlord about that leaky pipe?

Of course not! Until you're an adult, you don't own your own home or rent your own office space.

You have work and school and friends—probably more friends than most adults do—but you don't have your own place to hang. You're left to use public spaces as your own personal domain.

But available space is getting more and more difficult to find. Some people accuse businesses and urban designers of intentionally trying to shift teens off the street.

→ Sloped park benches and bus stop waiting areas discourage "loitering."

→ Studs on window ledges prevent anyone from perching there.

→ "Pig's ears," or metal ledges, keep skateboarders from using stairs and curbs.

→ Speakers play classical music to drive young people away.

→ Kids and teens can often hear at higher frequencies than adults. A small speaker called the Mosquito produces annoying high-pitched sounds only young people can hear.

Combined with surveillance cameras, all these strategies send a message: "You're not wanted." Sometimes, that message is even more blatant. In 1999, Britain passed a law that said any youth caught on camera while engaging in "antisocial behavior" could be banned from a park, a street, or a neighborhood. Antisocial behavior was anything that might cause "harassment, alarm, or distress" to other people. It included things like painting graffiti or being drunk in

public, but it also included more minor acts like loitering, asking for money, smoking, and spitting.

In 2014, the government changed the name of the law and tweaked a few details. But the offenses, including conduct that might cause "alarm or distress to any person," remained the same.

THE CREEPY LINE

THE NEXT MODEL ON THE CATWALK is sporting a tailored dress and ... a surgical mask? Once considered a polite way to stop the spread of germs, face masks have evolved into fashion statements on the streets of Tokyo. Trend-watchers have offered all sorts of reasons:

→ Japanese young people are used to communicating by phone or email, so they feel safer behind a visual "wall."

→ Wearers feel more alluring when only their eyes show.

→ The masks are a reaction against constant surveillance.

If that last one is true, the Japanese teens might be interested in the work of Chicago artist Leo Selvaggio. He created 3-D masks of his own face to help other people fool security cameras.

WHAT DO YOU THINK? Would you wear a mask to preserve your privacy? Would you wear someone else's face?

Malls and Morals

IS A MALL PRIVATE OR PUBLIC? Shoppers feel free to wander through the space, and the concourses are shared by many businesses. It seems like a city street that happens to have a roof. But once inside a mall, people are under surveillance. Cameras and security guards keep a close eye on visitors. And they probably watch some more than others.

In one study, researchers found that almost nine out of every ten times that security guards were called to an area of the mall, it was because of groups of young men. It's possible that all of these young men were committing crimes. But it's also possible that they looked rough, or they were making a lot of noise, or they were acting in a way that might deter other shoppers. Because as it turns out, a mall is *not* a public space. It's a privately owned space for buying and selling. The role of a security guard is to keep the mall an environment where buying and selling can happen smoothly.

The use of cameras inside malls—where shoppers feel as if they're in a public space but businesses feel that they're in charge—has led to all sorts of interesting moral questions.

In Britain, security guards have helped police use mall cameras to zoom in on the phones of suspected gang members or drug dealers, tracking the numbers they dialed. They've also followed suspicious-looking shoppers to the parking lot to photograph their license plates.

A study in Saudi Arabia showed that conservative security guards targeted young men who "chased females," wore Western-style clothes, or shopped during calls to prayer. The young men posed no security threat; the guards were simply influenced by their own religious and cultural beliefs.

In Canada, shoppers are supposed to be warned when they're on camera. But a study of two of the country's biggest malls showed that only a third of stores obeyed those privacy laws.

When it comes to mall security, it's *caveat emptor:* buyer beware.

NO SHIRT, NO SHOES ... NO SHOPPING?

IN MOST PLACES, it's legal for a business to refuse service ... as long as it's for a good reason. If an employee thinks you're being rowdy, disturbing other customers, or shoplifting, you can get the boot.

What stores *can't* do is discriminate against certain customers and not others. Which doesn't always stop staff from doing just that.

How far between your eyebrows? How wide is your nose? To recognize faces, computers analyze hundreds of tiny measurements. Those measurements are then used to create 3-D images. Like DNA information or fingerprints, a "faceprint" can be permanently stored.

In Australia in 2015, Apple employees were caught on camera ejecting a group of young black men from the store. The boys were in school uniforms and not causing trouble. After the incident, Apple apologized and promised better training for its staff.

LIBERTY ... SORT OF

IN 2013, a journalist named Ryan Gallagher called the U.S. National Park Service and two private security companies. All three threatened to sue him.

Ryan had asked about plans to use new facial recognition technology at the Statue of Liberty. Apparently, it was a touchy subject.

The type of surveillance camera used at many public sites today is shockingly high-tech.

Experts suggest that cameras and software at a destination like the Statue of Liberty can:

→ Spot unattended bags and backpacks, which might hide explosives

→ Count the people who arrive and depart, and flag anyone who stays behind

→ Tell the difference between an authorized ferry in the water around the statue, and an unauthorized boat

Many organizations don't release the details of their security plans, because that would make it easier for criminals or terrorists to thwart the systems. But as Ryan Gallagher pointed out, more than 3 million innocent visitors tour the Statue of Liberty each year—and they might want to know if their faces are tracked, stored, and shared. After all, the statue is an international symbol of freedom.

>ACTION ALERT< Concerned about public surveillance in your town or city? Check the websites of local politicians to see who is interested in issues of privacy. You may be too young to vote, but you're not too young to write letters, attend council meetings, or volunteer.

THE CREEPY LINE

SITES SUCH AS FACEBOOK AND SHUTTERFLY allow users to "tag," or label, the people in photographs. Using facial recognition technology, the sites can then automatically tag matching faces in other photos.

In 2015 and 2016, two groups launched class-action lawsuits in the U.S., saying that Facebook and Shutterfly were collecting and storing biometric data without asking permission first. One man complained that his friends had identified photos of him on Shutterfly. The site had searched for and labeled his face, when he wasn't even a Shutterfly user. Activists worry that information from this sort of random photo—the brand of soft drink the man prefers, for example, or the type of beach he likes to visit—could be sold for marketing purposes.

There are laws in some U.S. states to prevent companies from storing biometric data. But often, those laws exclude photographs.

WHAT DO YOU THINK? So ... who's right? Are Facebook and Shutterfly offering a harmless way to help sort photos, or are they invading people's privacy? How do you feel about your face being tagged and tracked?

NAME: CYNTHIA SMITH
AGE: 3 YEARS
EYE COLOUR: GREEN
HEIGHT: 3'5"
POTENTIAL FUTURE CRIMINAL.
DOES NOT PLAY WELL WITH OTHERS.

ADJUSTING THE FOCUS

STOP, THIEF! You're on camera!

A study in South Korea found that use of security cameras cut crime by almost half, while crime in streets not covered by cameras remained the same. But studies elsewhere have revealed different results. In the U.S., some studies found that when one neighborhood was closely watched, crime merely shifted a few blocks away.

Even if all the police departments in the world stopped using their own cameras, there would still be lenses peering at the streets from ATMs and convenience stores, traffic lights and government sites.

In 2014, representatives of 10 European cities decided that every security camera should be:

PRIVACY SAYS:

1. **LEGAL.** It should meet all local laws.

2. **NECESSARY.** Is crime increasing? Graffiti? An organization should be able to explain exactly why it needs a camera.

3. **PROPORTIONAL.** The type of camera should suit the space. There should be no need for facial recognition software in a playground, for example.

4. **TRANSPARENT.** The public should know the camera exists, who operates it, and why.

5. **ACCOUNTABLE.** The organization controlling the camera should take responsibility for the data collected.

6. **INDEPENDENTLY MONITORED.** Someone independent should be checking to see if all the rules are being followed.

7. **CITIZEN-FRIENDLY.** The public should have input into how cameras are used, and even help plan surveillance systems.

As more people become aware of the cameras watching them, and as more of our open spaces become less open, rules like these might help strike a balance between crime prevention and public freedom.

CAUGHT IN THE WEB

MORE THAN A BILLION people use Facebook. Add the users of other social media platforms, and the numbers grow even more staggering.

Most people use social media to stay informed and keep in touch with friends. Whether we're poking our long-lost cousins, signing petitions, or retweeting kitten pictures, we're offering something of ourselves. In a way, we're saying, "Hey, these are all the things I believe in. Do you think the same way? What do we have in common?"

Social media is all about sharing. It was designed to be that way. But it's possible to give away too much information. When things move from digital to real life, and from IP address to street address, sharing on the Internet can become a scary thing.

THE NEW FRONTIER

THE TENSION BETWEEN PUBLIC AND PRIVATE is nothing new. Two American lawyers, Louis Brandeis and Samuel Warren, were some of the first to delve into the idea.

> DUDE, I'M THINKING THERE'S, LIKE, ZONES OF PRIVACY. U KNOW?

> WAT?

> U GOT UR INNER CIRCLE, THINGS U NEVER SHARE.

> K

> THEN INTIMATE SECRETS, BFFS ONLY. AND STUFF U TELL ALL UR FRIENDS. THEN CASUAL CONVOS. SEE?

> KEWL

Okay, so that's not exactly how Louis and Samuel discussed their ideas, back in 1890. But they did see four distinct privacy "circles": secrets people kept to themselves; things they shared with a select few; things they told all of their friends; and conversations that could be overheard by anyone.

They were commenting partly on something that was, at the time, a new invention. It was seen as invasive, frightening, and quickly expanding. It was … Kodak photography.

Until 1888, photography had required large glass plates and heavy equipment. But when George Eastman introduced his first portable camera,

In the early 1900s, President Theodore Roosevelt suggested outlawing cameras in public parks, feeling people should be able to stroll without having their privacy invaded. In 2014, the U.S. National Park Service banned drones and model aircraft from all national parks—for very similar reasons.

preloaded with 100 negatives, it was suddenly possible to take snap-shots of everyday life. It was also possible for news photographers to accost the rich and famous on the street.

Just a few years after Louis and Samuel wrote their privacy article, a piece in the *New York Times* gasped that "Kodak fiends" were snap-ping pictures at every opportunity, then selling those shots to the tabloids. "All over the avenue the women are constantly brought face to face with a Kodak and snapped." And the prints, cried the newspaper, were sometimes far from flattering.

All that upset over snapshots may seem silly to us now, but those photos were the first way for other people or the media to invade someone's life, discover their secrets, and keep the evidence.

Privacy could no longer be taken for granted.

Snap Happy

EVEN AS CAMERAS BECAME COMMONPLACE, people continued to muse about the meanings of privacy. In 1960, a lawyer named William Prosser created America's first privacy law by pointing to four problem behaviors:

1. Intruding into someone's private affairs

2. Making embarrassing facts public

3. Creating false publicity

4. Using someone's name or picture without permission

Those issues still exist. Imagine someone took a photo of you on the field, then replaced the soccer ball with a kitten and published an article about your habit of kicking cats. That would be false publicity. If they pasted your name and photo into an advertisement for foot fungus without your permission, that would be using your image. Either way, you'd probably feel as if your privacy had been violated.

William's four categories of privacy were so clear and useful, they influenced lawmakers around the world. Countries from Angola to Argentina and Venezuela to Zimbabwe now have privacy laws.

But some experts argue that by defining privacy issues so precisely in 1960, William actually limited the law's ability to address threats from new kinds of technology.

The things we fear today are a little different from what people worried about half a century ago. How do traditional ideas about privacy apply to things like cyberbullying, identity theft, or social media monitoring? These are questions that people—and the courts—are still trying to answer.

SOCIAL MEDIA

FACEBOOK, TWITTER, TUMBLR, SNAPCHAT, YOUTUBE, Instagram. Anytime we post on a social media site, we're sharing information. Depending on our privacy settings, we may be sharing that information with a few friends, or with the whole world. But we're also providing exactly what the "Kodak fiends" were giving the tabloids more than a century ago: evidence.

The information we leave behind online is sometimes called our "digital tattoo." All that data is stuck to us forever, like permanent ink.

In many ways, social media is built on trust. If a guy shares his fears in a private message

to his friends, he's trusting them not to spread the word. If a girl sends a risqué photo to her boyfriend, she's trusting him not to forward it to his friends.

According to research, teens either have a lot of faith in their friends or they prefer not to imagine the things that could go wrong. The Pew Research Center is an American company that tracks Internet trends. In 2015, its surveys found that teens were sharing more information on social media than ever before:

privacy says:

→ Each post, each shared photo, travels to other people's screens.

→ Even if we erase something, it can live on in screen captures or reposts.

→ 91 percent of teens share photos.

→ More than 70 percent list the names. of their schools and hometowns.

→ About half post their email addresses.

→ One in five share their cellphone numbers.

Though only 9 percent of teens were concerned about how their online data was used, one in six had been approached online by a stranger who made them feel scared or uncomfortable.

violence gone viral

WHEN SHE WAS IN SEVENTH GRADE in Port Coquitlam, British Columbia, Amanda Todd began chatting with a man she'd met online. During one of their conversations, Amanda flashed her breasts at her webcam; he saved the image. Soon he was blackmailing her, insisting that she "give him a show" if she didn't want the picture made public.

Amanda refused, and the man followed through on his threat. He sent the photo to her family and friends. Later, someone set up a Facebook page featuring the image. Other online strangers began harassing her. The bullying carried over into Amanda's real life. She changed schools twice, attempting to escape the stories. Eventually, she attempted suicide.

Online and off, the bullying escalated. Hateful posts continued after Amanda posted a YouTube video, explaining with flashcards what she'd endured. They continued even after Amanda committed suicide in 2012.

A 35-year-old Dutch man was eventually arrested for stalking Amanda online and releasing her photo to the world. But the many others students and adults who participated in the cyberbullying faced no repercussions.

And in other parts of the world, there are other victims—people driven to extreme measures by online harassment:

→ A 14-year-old girl called Amnesia jumped from the top floor of an Italian hotel in 2014. After she had posted about breaking up with her boyfriend, people had left comments that said "Kill yourself" and "You are not normal."

→ Nineteen-year-old Australian Jessica Cleland killed herself in 2015 after vicious online bullying. The year before, the Australian Human Rights Commission had called for action after several other suicides were linked to cyberbullying. Complaints to the commission rose to 17,000 that year.

→ When 18-year-old Tyler Clementi kissed another man in his dorm room in New Jersey, his roommate secretly watched through a webcam, then posted about it on Twitter. The exposure may have been one of the factors that led Tyler to jump from the George Washington Bridge on September 22, 2010.

Researchers have tracked these sorts of privacy invasions and cyberbullying instances in Australia, Belgium, China, Germany, India, Ireland, Italy, Japan, Spain, Sweden, and Turkey. Not all victims kill themselves, of course, and people who commit suicide often have other emotional, social, or health issues in their lives. But cyberbullying can push vulnerable kids over the edge.

Once, people targeted by bullies at school could find refuge inside their own homes. But the Internet now allows bullies to continue their harassment everywhere, even inside kids' bedrooms, via 24-hour social media access. To victims, the abuse can seem never-ending and inescapable.

There are no easy solutions. One study in Finland showed that when teachers worked hard to stop bullying in their classrooms, students were *more* likely to target others online. Meanwhile, teachers and parents worry that cyberbullying can be done in a sort of code. For example, if a hashtag is created to represent someone, it can be used to say derogatory things without a real name ever being mentioned. That makes it harder for parents and teachers to intervene.

But many schools and police forces are slowly finding better ways to address online bullying. In recent cases, some police officers have borrowed the identities of victims, posing as kids online and chatting with a cyberbully until they could pinpoint the person in real life.

Technology may provide new solutions, too. In South Korea, a new service emails parents when their teens receive an instant message with words or inappropriate language. The idea is to have parents interfere early and possibly get their kids offline when bullying begins.

In 2014, an Illinois teen named Trisha Prabhu created a software program that detects potentially hurtful messages and prompts kids to think twice before posting. Trisha has given a TEDx talk about her invention, and showcased it at a White House science fair.

⋝ACTION ALERT⋜

If you ever find yourself the victim of a cyberbully, here are some good first steps:

→ **TAKE SCREENSHOTS,** print the conversation, or write notes about when and how the bullying occurred.

→ **BLOCK THE PERSON** from texting or calling you. Most social media sites have a function that lets you block and report abusive accounts.

→ **LOG OFF.**

→ **TELL A PARENT** or teacher, or call a kids' help line.

→ **IF SOMEONE IS THREATENING YOU,** harassing you, or invading your privacy, call the police.

THE CREEPY LINE

IN OHIO, NINTH-GRADE STUDENT Matthew Homyk struggled with a stutter, depression, and cutting. Several times, he'd landed in the hospital.

In 2013, Matthew went to his father with a new problem. He'd used a social media site called Ask.fm, which allows users to post questions. Some of the answers are anonymous, some of them not. Matthew was receiving nasty messages via the site, questioning his sexual orientation and mocking his mental illness, among other things. His dad encouraged him to log off the site forever, but Matthew couldn't stop reading the things other people were saying about him.

In January 2014, Matthew was hospitalized again. He committed suicide the night he was released.

WHAT DO YOU THINK? Matthew was already struggling with depression when the online abuse began. So, were the cyberbullies to blame for his suicide? Should the site's administrators have monitored the posts and removed things that were abusive? Or was Matthew simply unable to handle what many other kids would have brushed aside?

More Than Mischief

IN 2014, the Polk County Sheriff's Office in Florida received a call. The voice on the other end of the line said he was going to drive to Fort Meade High School in a black van and shoot everyone. Police leapt into action and locked down the school ... only to find the call was a hoax. That morning, an online gamer had sent a message to a girl that read, "I'm going to Swat your school."

When they receive a call about an extreme situation, the police respond with full force and specially trained officers—a SWAT team. Faking a situation that will prompt this sort of reaction is called "swatting." It's especially dangerous because officers arrive heavily armed and prepared for violence.

Police traced the Florida false alarm to a teen in Coquitlam, British Columbia. He later pled guilty to 23 charges. For a year, he'd wreaked havoc with swatting incidents across Canada and the United States. He'd even shut down Disneyland by calling in a bomb threat. The teen was sentenced to 16 months in jail.

Ask.fm was created by two brothers from Latvia. When they were growing up, Latvia was a tightly controlled Soviet state. The brothers wanted their social media site to allow kids a type of freedom that they never had.

Of course, swatting would be much more difficult if people revealed less personal information online. This particular gamer could never have sent the police to a girl's school if he didn't know where she lived.

Sometimes, people share this sort of information casually, without a second thought. While chatting on social media or playing an online game, they mention their school or their street name. Other times, hackers delve a little deeper to uncover addresses and phone numbers.

⋮ACTION ALERT⋮ However it's obtained, that sort of personal information is dangerous in the wrong hands. Which is why experts suggest certain safety rules for online communication:

→ **NEVER** give a stranger your full name, your address, or your phone number.

→ **NEVER** share your passwords.

→ **NEVER** share real-life plans with an online friend.

→ **NEVER** meet an online friend in real life without telling your parents first.

Those are rules simple enough to be explained to six- and seven-year-old kids as they log onto Minecraft servers for the first time. But they're also rules that teens and adults too often forget.

STRIKE THREE

DID YOU HAVE AN "ALL ABOUT ME" BOOK when you were a kid? Somewhere to write down your age, address, hair color, parents' names, and more? To an experienced hacker, our online profiles often read just like those books. We provide our email address on one site, post our phone number on a second, and upload pictures of our school basketball team on a third. It doesn't take long for someone to put together a profile.

When someone's personal information is uncovered online and then released to the world, it's called "doxxing." The word comes from "dox," an abbreviation for "documents." Often, doxxing happens when people decide someone's online behavior warrants public punishment. Maybe a hacker releases the home phone number of an unethical corporate executive and asks everyone to start dialing. Maybe an online group gets tired of a troll's hateful messages and doxxes the troublemaker. Even politicians have doxxed their opponents. In 2015, U.S. presidential candidate Donald Trump read an opponent's cellphone number on national television.

Some people say that in order to cut down on hateful online messages, everyone should be required to use their real names when they post comments. Other people say anonymity allows us to be more honest and the Internet should be all about complete freedom of speech.

Though it's usually legal, doxxing is a form of harassment. It creates huge headaches for the victims, and can sometimes lead to safety concerns. Would you want everyone in the country calling your cell? Or turning up at your door?

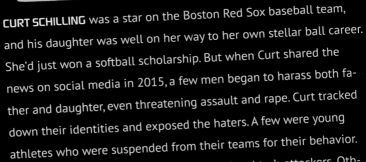

THE CREEPY LINE

CURT SCHILLING was a star on the Boston Red Sox baseball team, and his daughter was well on her way to her own stellar ball career. She'd just won a softball scholarship. But when Curt shared the news on social media in 2015, a few men began to harass both father and daughter, even threatening assault and rape. Curt tracked down their identities and exposed the haters. A few were young athletes who were suspended from their teams for their behavior.

Many applauded Curt for doxxing his daughter's attackers. Others said he overreacted to comments meant to remain anonymous.

WHAT DO YOU THINK? Should people be held responsible for everything they say online? And is doxxing always wrong, or can it be used for good?

REVENGE 2.0

PSYCHOLOGY STUDENT HOLLY JACOBS and her boyfriend took explicit pictures while they were dating. Then, when the two broke up in 2009, the boyfriend began publishing them online—along with Holly's email address and details about her life and her work. Holly found herself in the center of a storm of abuse.

She hired a lawyer. She visited three different police stations, looking for someone to take her situation seriously. She approached the FBI. She worked with an Internet expert to try to find her photos on the web and remove them.

When none of her efforts worked, Holly founded the Cyber Civil Rights Initiative, which provides support to harassment victims, works with social media sites on fair policies, and helps draft legislation.

In Europe, lawmakers have recently declared that everyone should have "the right to be forgotten." People can complete a form on the Google website, for example, and request that damaging posts or photos be removed from search-engine results. If that doesn't work, there are data-protection agencies in each country that can take search-engine companies to court.

That process isn't easy, and finding embarrassing photos on the Internet is like finding leaves in a forest—there's no shortage. Obviously, life would be easier if we all avoided posting cringeworthy things in the first place.

TAKING THE BAIT

CLICK.

Wow! This website's offering free cruises. All you have to do is enter your name and address, and you're guaranteed to win.

Click.

Oops ... there's a small tax issue. But you're going to win an entire cruise in exchange, right? You'll just type in your government ID number and *voilà!*

The bad news? There's no free cruise coming your way. The worse news? You've just given away all your personal information to someone who's phishing—basically, "fishing" for your personal details.

Most of us are smart enough not to accept free cruise offers, but phishing can take more subtle forms. Sometimes we receive emails that look as if they're from a site where we regularly shop, or a place we regularly bank. But they're fakes! A few clicks later, we're potential victims of identity theft.

Identity theft involves stealing someone's personal information, including their government ID numbers, then posing as that person to open credit card accounts or apply for loans. Sometimes, criminals gather the information they need online. Other times, they steal real-life tax forms from mailboxes.

Kids are tempting targets for identity theft because often, no one notices the problem for months or years. Meanwhile, someone has applied for loans and racked up credit card charges in the kid's name.

ACTION ALERT Experts say:

→ **KEEP GOVERNMENT ID INFO** secret from everyone.

→ **CHECK ONLINE** to see if you have a credit rating.

Unless you have your own credit cards, you shouldn't have a credit rating. If you do, maybe someone else has gone phishing in the wrong pond.

HIRED AND FIRED

THERE'S THAT ONE EMBARRASSING PHOTO of you giving the finger to the camera. And okay, so maybe your spelling isn't perfect when you're online. But do these things really matter? In 2014, researchers asked this question to a large group of business students and the students said, "No. No one cares."

Then the researchers approached companies who might hire recent business graduates. Would rude online photos or bad spelling make them rethink hiring decisions? The businesses overwhelmingly said yes.

More and more, people's online activities are affecting their real lives. In 2011, Taylor Bell was a senior student at Itawamba Agricultural High School in Mississippi. He was suspended after writing and performing a rap, then posting it to Facebook and YouTube. Taylor's lyrics accused two school coaches of having relationships with female students. He used racially charged language and threatened the coaches with violence.

According to the school, the allegations were false and the rap lyrics were threats. Taylor said his suspension was equal to censorship, and the references to violence in his lyrics were common rap techniques, not real threats.

Taylor's case highlights a question being raised at more and more schools. Can students be punished for things they say or do outside of school hours and off school grounds? Some districts in the United States have hired companies to scan all student social media use for signs of bullying or depression. At other schools, athletes have found their accounts monitored to ensure nothing they say online can tarnish their team's reputation.

In Mississippi, Taylor lost his first court case against the school, but won an appeal in 2014. The appeals court said Taylor had recorded and posted his rap entirely off campus, and his actions hadn't caused any serious disruption at the school. He was vindicated—but only long after he'd graduated from an alternative high school.

security says:
Schools have a right to monitor their students. Besides, they're doing it for the students' own safety.

privacy says:
Students can't speak freely knowing the coach or the principal is watching over their online shoulder.

TECHNOLOGY TOOLBOX

CHECK MESSAGE. ANSWER. DELETE. CHECK. ANSWER. DELETE.

That's one way teens have found to keep their messages private. It's not foolproof, of course. There's nothing to keep the recipient from snapping a screenshot. But it does prevent a nosy parent from picking up the cell and scrolling through old messages.

Research has shown that kids and teens are also very careful about who accesses certain information. While they might share risky

photos or posts, they do so only with people they trust. And finally, kids and teens often manage several different online profiles so they can maintain separate personas.

→ My parents have friended me on Facebook. Ack! I'll move my private conversations with friends to Snapchat.

→ I love to quilt but my friends think it's dorky. I'll set up a separate Tumblr to keep in touch with my fellow stitchers.

→ I only want to connect with a few people. I'll use my middle name or a pseudonym so I can't be found as easily.

Do these strategies work? Not always. Should we all be more careful than we are? Probably. But are adults correct when they say kids don't care about privacy? Absolutely not. A British study found that 95 percent of teens had adjusted their privacy settings on Facebook, compared to only 65 percent of all users. Studies of American and Australian teens found the same: young people were more, not less, concerned about security than the average adult. Teens wanted to discuss certain things without eavesdropping adults present, and they wanted to portray a certain image to potential schools or employers.

We all—kids, teens, and adults alike—instinctively understand the privacy zones defined by Louis and Samuel in the 1800s. We all know that some things are best kept secret. But we haven't always found the perfect ways to translate those ideals to the online world.

⇒ACTION ALERT⇐

The best posting rules are the following:

→ **DOUBLE CHECK BEFORE YOU POST.** Ask yourself if the post portrays you accurately, if it could be used to hurt you, or if you would be upset if it were shared.

→ **REMEMBER THE DIGITAL TATTOO:** Anything online can last forever.

→ **KEEP PASSWORDS SECRET, ALWAYS,** as well as ID and addresses.

And here's the advice given to people who find themselves the target of online abuse:

→ **KEEP YOUR COOL** and don't take revenge.

→ **BLOCK USERS** and increase your privacy using the site's settings, if possible.

→ **REPORT THE ABUSE** to the site itself.

→ **REPORT THE PROBLEM** to parents, teachers, or the police.

SHOP 'TIL YOU DROP DATA

WHAT IF A FORENSICS TEAM combed the mall for evidence we'd left behind? They might find a hair in a changing room or a fingerprint on a counter. As TV crime shows have taught us, we leave bits of ourselves wherever we go.

The same rule applies online. Companies tracking our online activities can find our birthdates, middle names, clothing sizes, color preferences, and relationship statuses, and the amount of cash we have to spend.

How?

Well, shopping's not just about style anymore.

BULL'S-EYE

IN 2012, the *New York Times Magazine* broke this story: A father had stormed into a Target store in Minneapolis, furious that the retailer had sent his teenage daughter coupons for maternity clothes and baby supplies. The man accused the store manager of encouraging teen pregnancy.

The manager apologized, and called the man at home a few days later to tell him once again just how sorry he was. But by then, Dad had changed his tone. "I had a talk with my daughter," he said. "It turns out there's been some activities in my house I haven't been completely aware of. She's due in August. I owe you an apology."

Ten years before this story was published, Target hired a statistician named Andrew Pole and asked him to figure out a way to tell when customers were pregnant. After all, people shopping for babies spend a lot of money, and might go on to buy toys, children's clothes, school supplies ... The opportunities for advertising seemed endless. And why send all its customers brochures for playpens if Target could send brochures *only* to those with small children?

Like many other department stores, Target offers loyalty cards. When you buy something and the cashier swipes your loyalty card, you earn points. In exchange, the store gets a record of all your purchases. Target also offers a baby registry. Once parents sign up with their due date, friends can buy them gifts from their wish list.

Andrew, the clever statistician, began his search for preggo cus-

tomers by matching baby-registry
names to loyalty-card
holders. That gave
him a list of shoppers
who were definitely
pregnant. Then he
analyzed the products
bought by those women.
He found certain patterns:

→ Moms-to-be bought more lotion.

→ Early in their pregnancies, they bought
   vitamins.

→ Closer to their due dates, they shopped for washcloths and
   cotton balls.

By analyzing statistics like these then searching for those
patterns in Target's loyalty-card records, Andrew learned to predict
which Target shoppers were pregnant—*even* when they weren't in
the baby registry. Now the store could send flyers and coupons for
baby supplies directly to those women.

When this story went public, people were shocked to learn
how closely Target was watching their shopping habits. But Target
wasn't the first or the last company to put its customers under
the microscope.

DUDE, WHERE'S MY DATA?

TO MARKETERS, the world is all about connections. All a company needs to do is figure out who's buying hockey sticks. Then it can sell more helmets. If it creates a list of customers buying books about breakups, it can sell that list to a company selling super-sized ice-cream tubs. To marketers, the world is all about connections.

Through loyalty cards and credit cards, customer surveys, and data bought from other companies, stores learn a lot about us. If you've ever signed up for a loyalty card at your local mall, you probably provided your name, age, address, and gender. From your address alone, a store can look at your neighborhood and guess certain things about you:

→ How much money your family earns

→ How far you drive to shop

→ What school you go to

→ Maybe even your ethnicity

Once it tracks your shopping for a few weeks or months, the company can guess even more:

→ What you like to read

→ Whether you throw parties often

→ Whether you've gone on a diet this year

There are huge companies dedicated to collecting information about people. Those companies track our online activities and buying patterns. So, what if our local department store buys data from one of those companies and adds the information to its collection? Now the store knows:

→ Which social media sites you visit

→ How many friends you have online

→ What religious or political groups you join

In fact, the store may know you better than you know yourself.

Every time you swipe a loyalty card, click "like" on a website, or choose a movie on Netflix, you generate computer data. IBM estimates that many American companies store at least 100 terabytes (100,000 gigabytes) of information. Each!

Most of this data is of no use to humans. What person could read and make sense of 100,000 gigabytes? But a computer can. When a computer sorts through masses of information to find patterns, that's called "data mining." And data mining is worth millions of dollars.

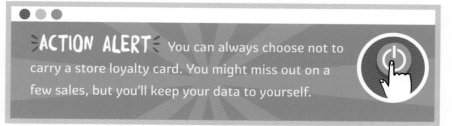

ACTION ALERT You can always choose not to carry a store loyalty card. You might miss out on a few sales, but you'll keep your data to yourself.

IF YOU'RE HAPPY AND THEY KNOW IT

IMAGINE IF YOUR PHONE BUZZED while you were browsing the racks, with a text message from the store itself. "We see you've viewed our brooms and hats," it might say. "May we suggest the black cats in aisle six?"

Dutch researchers used special cameras to watch how customers traveled through a large store. By tracking the shoppers' head movements, the researchers could tell that most shoppers went through a four-step process:

1. **ORIENTATION.** "Oh, cosmetics are on the second floor."

2. **SELECTION.** "Which wart cream is more effective? Which is cheaper?"

3. **APPRECIATION.** "Are warts really a problem? Do I need to spend my cash on cream?"

4. **DECISION MAKING.** "Yup—ring me up!"

By gathering information like this, stores can tell whether or not most customers are happy with the selection of products being offered. They can track the most popular routes, and place special displays along the way. Computers could even select customers to target with personalized advertisements.

"We notice you own a frog. Don't forget our cauldrons, second floor!"

THE CREEPY LiNE

YOU'RE BEING FOLLOWED. As you walk through the store, lenses swivel and computers calculate. They can tell whether you're a kid or an adult, whether you're male or female. They track how long you linger at the coffee counter and what you buy. They notice which displays you browse. And if you return the following week, they add new information to your existing profile.

How? More and more stores are using cameras and facial recognition technology, as well as tracking their customers' cell-phone signals. It doesn't matter if your phone is connected—as long as it's set to detect Wi-Fi signals, the store can trace and identify it to find out whether you're a repeat shopper.

WHAT DO YOU THINK? Is it weird to be watched? Or do stores need surveillance data to help them compete with online retailers?

WHAT DOES THE FRY SAY?

YUM ... CURLY FRIES! Did you just click "like" on those potato pics? If so, you might be more intelligent than average.

In 2013, researchers at the University of Cambridge proved they could predict the personalities of Facebook users by tracking only their "likes." The researchers watched volunteers' Facebook clicks, then had those people complete surveys, personality tests, and intelligence tests. Without even reading people's comments or analyzing their posts, the researchers were able to draw surprisingly accurate conclusions. Here are a few of the study's more wacky findings:

→ People who "liked" Hello Kitty were more open than average, but less emotionally stable. They were more likely to be liberal, Christian, and slightly younger than the average Facebook user.

→ When Facebook users "liked" statements about committed relationships (*I'm with you, so I don't want anybody else*), it was more likely that their parents had divorced while the user was a child.

→ People who "liked" thunderstorms or science stories were more likely to have high intelligence.

It makes sense that smart people like science stories. But some connections seemed entirely random. Why would curly fries act as signals of high IQ?

Maybe spirals attract smart people. More likely, there's a sort of "social contagion" at work. When you have a cold (*achoo!*), you pass your germs along to others (*gesundheit*). And when you "like" something (*achoo!*), your preferences are shown to your family and friends. They might rub off on those people (*gesundheit*). Smart people tend to hang out with other smart people, so maybe the brainiac world is just one big festival of curly fries.

Data Overload

SITES LIKE FACEBOOK make money by selling advertising. Really, they're selling *you*. They're saying: *Hey, advertise with us! We have access to all the cool kids.* To help sell ads, they gather information about their users and package that information for companies. *You're launching a new line of cute puppy fashion? Please, let us place your banner ad on our three million accounts of dog lovers.*

As the Cambridge researchers showed, our social media activities can be used to accurately predict our genders, sexual orientations, and political views. All of that information allows companies to precisely target their ads. And that can be scary.

→ If you ever suffer from a drug or alcohol addiction, your social media history will reflect that information.

→ Social media sites may know that users are homosexual before those people are ready to share the news.

→ Political parties can pay to advertise to specifically chosen accounts. In the United States, Republican candidates might send ads to people who support the right to carry guns; Democratic candidates might target people who "like" environmental posts.

Obfuscation via kitten: While officers in Brussels, Belgium, searched for terrorists in 2015, they asked residents not to tweet about police activities. Belgians took those instructions one step further. They flooded the #BrusselsLockdown hashtag with cat pictures, so anyone posting about police would be lost in the feline frenzy.

What if you'd like to keep parts of yourself private?

Most of us click the "like" button as if it's no big deal. But privacy activists say that with every click, we're giving away our secrets.

On the other hand, there are ways to skew the results—sometimes by accident. You might be shopping for tea cozies for your aunt, and find yourself receiving ads for yarn stores. You can also confuse comp-uter tracking on purpose. There are programs you can download that work in the background of your browser, automatically clicking on random ads. There are so many of those random clicks, they disguise your real online activities. In technical terms, this is called "obfuscation" —obscuring real information.

KNITTING KNEWS

A WORD FROM OUR KNITTER OF THE MONTH, DORIS:

TRACKING OURSELVES

HOW MANY TIMES did you brush your teeth last year? How many times did you floss? Do you exercise regularly? What's your resting heart rate? How many calories did you consume yesterday, and how many did you burn?

Smartphones (along with the Fitbit, the Jawbone UP, and other personal monitoring devices) allow people to collect data about themselves. Often, they do this as a self-improvement exercise. They count the number of steps they take each day to improve their fitness. They tally pushups, hoping for the perfect pectorals. They track their sleep, spending habits, or caffeine intake. Parents even track their babies' poops.

Personal tracking devices aren't always as private as they seem. In 2001, Fitbit users who hadn't properly read their privacy settings found out their, um, intimate bedroom moments were being counted—online! (Fitbit quickly put a stop

security says:
It's good to encourage yourself to improve. This sort of tracking could create a fitness revolution.

privacy says:
Companies like Google, Apple, or Fitbit might start selling our personal data to marketing companies.

to that.) In 2014, Jawbone collected sleep data from its California users and published it, to show how earthquakes affected sleep. No names were attached, but many users were still shocked—they hadn't known their data could be shared.

In the tech world, a "macroscope" is a computer system that collects tiny data points then analyzes them. Today, almost two billion people (and at least 40 percent of North American teens) carry macroscopes—smartphones—in their pockets.

THE CREEPY LINE

YOU'RE HEADING OUT for a walk when you notice a small robot hovering above your house. Slowly, the machine descends. It scans the exterior of your home, adjusts its position slightly, and drops a package at your front door. Inside, you find the shirt you ordered online a few hours before.

Science fiction? Nope. A mini-aircraft in Singapore delivered a letter and T-shirt in 2015, marking the first time mail had been delivered by drone. In Singapore, new laws allow drones to deliver packages, as long as the machines meet certain safety standards. Companies are lobbying to get the same permissions in North America.

WHAT DO YOU THINK? Do people really want robots flying above the streets? And how much information will those drones collect? With a little facial recognition software added, they could track what time we leave our homes, where we walk, where we shop, and when we return.

THE INTERNET OF THINGS

BRAD WAS THE CUTE ITALIAN STAR of a 2014 design show. But he wasn't some TV celebrity or famous decorator. No, Brad was a toaster.

Designer Simone Rebaudengo connected Brad and four of his toaster friends to the Internet and programmed them to compare their levels of use. When Brad was used less than his friends, he would wiggle his handle. If that didn't work and he was ignored for too long, Brad would list himself for sale on the Internet.

Brad was an exaggerated case, created to point out the strange ways our Internet use is expanding. But he has lots in common with new cars, house alarms, pacemakers, thermostats, televisions, and vending machines. They're all online. It's a phenomenon called "the Internet of Things," a phrase coined by a British tech guru named Kevin Ashton in 1999.

Some of these devices have obvious benefits:

→ Connected devices can leave us vulnerable. In 2014, a team of hackers showed they could access a networked thermostat in less than 15 seconds, then use the information from that thermostat to gain access to all the wireless activity in someone's house.

→ Computers aren't perfect. In January 2016, a software glitch shut down the connected thermostats in some North American homes—right in the middle of a winter cold snap.

→ Wired products could deliver our personal information to stores and marketing companies. For example, if your connected home showed that your thermostat was turned up and your TV on longer than usual, you might receive ads for cold medicine.

People are also coming up with creative uses for online machines. At a Maker Faire in Brooklyn in 2015, hackers were challenged to find new ways to use an Internet-connected fridge. The winning team designed a sharing basket. The Wi-Fi–connected basket sits inside your fridge with a tiny camera attached. When you have extra food—too many eggs, leftover lasagna—you pop it in your basket. Then the friends and neighbors on your sharing-basket app can check out the contents and pop by to pick up what they'd like.

But sharing isn't everything. Experts have some serious concerns about the Internet of Things.

Experts say that by 2020, there will be 50 billion devices feeding information to the Internet, creating 44 zettabytes of data. (A zettabyte is one sextillion bytes, or one trillion gigabytes. In non-mathematical terms, it's ... a lot.)

Through our real-life browsing habits, our online "likes," or even through our refrigerators, marketers are looking for information. How much do we want to provide?

→ Do we want our fridge tracking and sharing our food data, or would we rather stick with an old-fashioned fridge and a shopping list?

→ If our thermostats and electricity meters are connected to the Internet, could criminals figure out when we're home and when we're not?

→ Should companies need to earn a "seal of approval" from an organization that assesses privacy policies and data sharing?

Internet-connected products are optional. We're not forced to buy toys with webcams or door locks that can be accessed via smartphone. At some point, we shoppers need to decide where to draw the line between perks and privacy.

THE BIG BROTHER BOTHER

THERE ARE ALMOST THREE BILLION PEOPLE on the Internet. In North America, more than 95 percent of kids between the ages of 12 and 17 are online. More than 80 percent of them use social media. And all of those kids, along with their parents, grandparents, friends and teachers and the random strangers they pass on the street, are tracked by government agencies:

→ Countries including France, Germany, New Zealand, the United States and Canada collect data from citizens' emails and phone calls, and can store that data for years.

→ At times, the United States's National Security Agency (NSA) has collected and stored about two billion emails and phone calls a day. In 2015, it promised to stop such widespread surveillance of U.S. citizens.

→ Canada has pioneered software that allows governments to track anyone in the world who uses file-sharing websites for photos, music, videos, and documents.

→ The government of China requires all Internet providers to track the dates and times that users access the Internet, the users' account numbers, and the addresses of all websites visited.

→ Russia's security forces eavesdrop on more than half a million emails and phone calls each year.

In 1949, a British author named George Orwell published a book called *Nineteen Eighty-Four*. The society within the book is entirely controlled by an all-seeing government. Citizens can be watched at any time, and thinking for themselves is considered "thoughtcrime."

Some people say that the mass surveillance used by governments today is uncomfortably close to the frightening fictional world created in *Nineteen Eighty-Four* more than half a century ago.

SUPERHERO/SPY

PEOPLE STARTED PAYING MORE ATTENTION to government surveillance in 2013. That's when an American government contract worker named Edward Snowden quit his job, boarded a plane for Hong Kong, and contacted several journalists. He gave those journalists thousands of secret documents. Some of the files explained exactly how the U.S. government tracked its citizens.

THE CREEPY LINE

THEY'RE CALLED the most persecuted people on Earth. The Muslim Rohingya in western Myanmar (Burma) are persecuted by neighboring Buddhist ethnic groups. The Rohingya are attacked by mobs, exiled from their villages, and forced to act as slaves for the military.

Tens of thousands flee across the border to Bangladesh. But in 2011, the government there began tracking its population with national identification cards—and the Rohingya aren't eligible. Without cards, the Rohingya can't send their children to school or find legitimate work.

Human rights activists say that Bangladesh should act more like Malaysia, where refugees are given United Nations ID cards allowing them to stay in the country. But according to UNICEF, 26 million Bangladeshi children live in poverty. The country doesn't want to encourage more arrivals.

WHAT DO YOU THINK? What should Bangladesh do? When governments track and count their citizens, does that give them the right to exclude non-citizens? What about the Rohingya people fleeing Myanmar with no ID at all? What are their options?

Traitor! The government has to hide its surveillance, or criminals and terrorists will know they're being watched. By revealing state secrets, Edward endangered his country.

One month after he left the country, Edward was charged with spying and stealing information. He fled to Russia, where he now lives in hiding. Meanwhile, Edward's documents continue to make the news and privacy activists continue to argue with government officials.

What's the answer? No one knows for sure. Even the U.S. courts are still debating the rights and wrongs of this sort of surveillance.

privacy says:

Hero! In a democracy, people must exchange information freely—to trade ideas without fear. Edward helped save society by revealing the surveillance.

Dragnets and Dog Doo-Doo

SECURITY FORCES SAY: Better safe than sorry. They'd rather scan all activities, all emails, all phone calls, than scan only a few and risk missing terrorist threats. But privacy activists point to three major problems with tracking and scanning:

1. **PAST ABUSES.** In 1933, the Belgian colonial government in Rwanda gave out ID cards that listed ethnicity. Based on family heritage, everyone was labeled Tutsi, Hutu, or Twa. The Belgians promoted the Tutsi people, giving them more access to power and wealth. The divide between the groups grew until 1994, when a Hutu-controlled government ordered all Tutsis killed—using ID cards to streamline the process. More than half a million people were killed in the genocide.

2. **INNOCENT BYSTANDERS.** In 2009, British protesters took the police to court after discovering that photos of law-abiding demonstrators were being kept on file. Three years later, a 12-year-old boy took the police to court for similar reasons. He'd been arrested then released without charges, but his photos had been kept—just in case.

3. **USELESS DATA.** The phone and Internet records collected by the United States NSA haven't actually prompted any arrests. Terrorists and criminals caught by the NSA have all been found through tips, investigations, or other traditional police tactics.

PRIVACY SAYS:

To prove just how much personal information is collected and sold, Maclean's magazine journalists bought Canada's privacy commissioner's phone records. They purchased the list online from an American data broker for about $200 U.S.

STOP ANIMAL CRUELTY!

Activists also worry about something called "surveillance creep." Once technology exists, it's easy to use it in new ways. Computer programs designed to track terrorists can be expanded to sift through all citizens' emails. While DNA databases were once used to track only convicted criminals, some police forces now store DNA samples from people even briefly suspected of crimes. Cameras designed to catch violent acts are easy to aim at teenagers who shouldn't be smoking, or dog-walkers who fail to scoop the poop.

CRIME TIME

CONVICTED OF COMMITTING A CRIME in the *future*? Does that seem like wacky science fiction? Well, more and more cities are using something called "predictive policing." In 2014, officials in Rochester, Minnesota, launched a program to find and rehabilitate future criminals, while they were still kids. First, the city studied convicted offenders. They created a list of childhood actions that many criminals had in common—things like skipping school and underage drinking. Then, the officials made a list of today's troublemaking truants. They didn't arrest those students. But they did refer them to programs for at-risk kids.

In situations like this one, some people worry that information gathering might go beyond school attendance rates. With the technology and data now available, city police could start analyzing high school transcripts, employment records, web-surfing behaviors, and even Fitbit scores.

Could our heart rates reveal aggressive personalities? And should we be held accountable before we've acted? Those are questions that privacy activists and police forces are still debating.

card tricks

YOU'RE WALKING HOME from a friend's birthday party when a police cruiser pulls up beside you and briefly flicks its siren. An officer asks you for ID, then enters your personal information into her computer. A few more questions and you're sent on your way ... completely innocent, but feeling like a criminal.

You've just been "carded."

Carding is the practice of stopping random people and entering their information into police databases.

In 2013, a judge ruled that when police stopped and frisked people on New York streets, it was unconstitutional, and sometimes a form of racial profiling. Black people were more likely to be targeted than white people. Similarly, a Columbia University study found that one-third of Muslim students in New York had been stopped by police and believed it was because of racial profiling.

It doesn't happen just in New York. A newspaper investigation in Toronto showed that more than a quarter of all people carded in 2013 were black, even though black people make up less than 10 percent of the population. In 2014, the city's police board put restrictions on the practice.

SAVE THE EARTH! OR NOT

IN 2003, a man named Mark Stone joined a British environmental organization. He became a trusted part of the group, even dating one of the other members. In 2009, he and the other activists planned to sneak inside a power plant and temporarily shut it down to protest the use of coal. But before the action took place, police raided protesters' homes, arresting 114 people.

It turned out that Mark Stone was an undercover police officer, aka Mark Kennedy. He'd traveled to 22 countries with environmental activists and participated in all sorts of demonstrations— feeding information to police the whole time. Other members of his environmental group were livid. And so was his girlfriend! It turned out that Mark had a wife and children in Ireland.

When the activists claimed that Mark had actually helped plan their power-plant demonstration, the court case against the environmentalists collapsed. So all his years of spying proved useless— except to warn activists that police were watching.

The British case wasn't the only one of its kind. In the United States, officials have been accused of infiltrating mosques to look for possible terrorists. In Canada, the government has spied on environmental and First Nations groups, even planting spies within groups that have been entirely peaceful in their protests.

THE CREEPY LINE

IN 2007, FBI AGENTS sent a link to a crime suspect's MySpace page. It was a fake news story about bomb threats. When the 15-year-old MySpace user opened the story, it secretly planted tracking software on his computer. Soon, the FBI was able to confirm the student's Internet address and location. Officers arrested the teen for making multiple bomb threats at his high school.

Bomb threats are serious business, and the officers successfully caught their suspect. On the other hand, they tricked him. And more important, they used a fake news story to do it. Many journalists worried that government spies posing as newspaper reporters could create a dangerous level of distrust—how would people know whether or not to believe the news?

WHAT DO YOU THINK? So ... were those FBI tactics sneaky, underhanded spying, or were they necessary law enforcement?

RIGHT BACK ATCHA

REMEMBER THE PANOPTICON, the prison with a central tower to allow guards to watch prisoners at any time? A French computer-science professor named Jean-Gabriel Ganascia has suggested a term for our new age: the catopticon. Named for catoptrics, the study of reflection and mirrors, the catopticon is a place where the act of watching works both ways.

Once, most security cameras belonged to governments, businesses, and police forces. Now, millions of people carry smartphone cameras in their pockets. Teenagers can expose an abusive teacher on YouTube; bystanders can upload video of a heavy-handed cop; activists can film their protests to prove that they're behaving peacefully.

There's another word for this sort of watching. Computer engineering professor Steve Mann calls it "sousveillance," or "watching below." He suggests that sousveillance is a reaction to surveillance, and if police and governments use one form while citizens use the other, we might all end up in a state of "equiveillance": everyone watching everyone else.

passport, please

IN 2013, 13-year-old Lucy and 11-year-old Ben were whisked away by security guards at an airport in Tunisia. They were on their way to a resort with their family, but it turned out their mother, Sally Jones, shared the same name as a suspected terrorist. The kids were held for nine hours before they and their parents were finally released.

When people travel across borders, they give up some personal privacy. Think about air travel, for example. Ticket, passport, luggage X-ray, laptop check, pat-down, body scan: passengers offer personal information at each of these stages.

After the terrorist attacks on New York's World Trade Center on September 11, 2001, 93 percent of Americans said they would give up some privacy to feel more secure, and 65 percent were in favor of full-body scanners in airports.

Following terrorist attacks on subway trains in London, 71 percent of British citizens said that all passengers should be required to carry ID, if that would increase security. And 79 percent said that police should be able to hold terror suspects for up to a week without necessarily charging them.

But increased security measures aren't the only possible responses to terrorist attacks. After the September 11, 2001, terrorist attacks in New York, and the attack at the *Charlie Hebdo* magazine offices in Paris in 2015, citizens in those countries called for greater unity. More people than ever before felt "favorable" toward their Muslim neighbors. When terrorists again targeted Paris in November 2015, there was a 20 percent increase in first-aid class enrollment, and officials had to turn away people lining up to donate blood.

THE CREEPY LINE

MANY COUNTRIES require a signed letter from parents before a child is allowed to cross a border without both parents present. It's a way to keep tabs on kids and reduce kidnappings.

In Saudi Arabia, the government has used technology to draw much stricter boundaries. Women in that country are legally considered minors throughout their lives. It's illegal for a woman to travel without the permission of her *mahram*, or male guardian. That guardian can be a father, a husband, a brother, or even a son.

In 2012, the nation launched a program that tracked people through their cellphones and sent texts to the *mahram* if a woman left the country. After much international protest, the program was suspended in 2014. But the idea left questions.

WHAT DO YOU THINK? How far should cellphone tracking go, and what if people other than kids and parents start setting our GPS boundary rules?

SCIENCE IN THE SEWER

WHAT A STINKER! Researchers in Cambridge, Massachusetts, are tracking toilet water. They say that by analyzing sewage, they can detect rates of drug use and disease. That can help doctors react quickly to address health problems in different parts of the city.

It's just one of the ways people have found to track the health of citizens. Here are some others:

→ People send fewer texts when they have fevers. So monitoring the number of text messages can serve as an early-warning system for flu outbreaks.

→ By tagging doctors, nurses, and equipment with RFID tags, researchers can track the ways bacteria might move around a hospital. If one patient gets an infection, the system can see which other patients could be at risk.

→ In 2014, Crisis Text Line released its data about when American teens were most likely to seek help. For example, those with anorexia often called on Mondays. And teens were most likely to feel depressed and isolated late at night.

Understanding when and where people need help is obviously a huge benefit. But when does health data become problematic? Could having records on file cause problems for kids in the future, when they look for jobs, travel, or apply for insurance? Could people's health information be stolen? The answers change as health care and big data come together.

ACTION ALERT Organizations such as Amnesty International and PEN International work to protect people who are unfairly targeted by government surveillance and censorship. These organizations often need volunteers for things like letter-writing campaigns.

If you're concerned about surveillance, do some research into privacy laws. Write to the editor of your local paper, outlining your concerns. And write to your political representatives, too.

people power

ACCESS TO TECHNOLOGY works both ways. It can help governments track people, but it can also help people evade authority.

In 2008, 16-year-old Li Shufen left her rural Chinese school with three friends. When her body was found in the river, the police said Li Shufen had committed suicide by jumping from a bridge.

The girl's family believed that she'd been assaulted and killed by the other teens, and that those teens had family connections to local officials, who were covering up her murder. Normally, there would have been no way to protest this under China's authoritarian rules.

But cellphone use had recently exploded throughout China. Over half of citizens now owned cellphones. After the murder, text messages began popping up across the community. Soon, 10,000 people showed up at a march to protest the failed investigation. Police vehicles and government buildings were vandalized.

Normally, this kind of event would have earned swift punishment in China. But this time, cellphones changed everything:

→ The phones allowed citizens to communicate openly in ways not previously possible.

→ They allowed news to spread quickly, to many people.

→ Because multiple people sent multiple messages, no lead organizers could be arrested or imprisoned.

→ The phones allowed photos and videos to be broadcast to news media in other parts of the world.

Activists in China have pointed to this incident—one that occurred in a poor rural community, far from technological or political hubs— to argue that China's government and police forces can no longer watch and control citizens the way they once did.

That doesn't mean all posting is safe. Thousands of people were arrested in July 2015 in an initiative to "clean the Internet." Authorities didn't explain the charges, but many activists believed people were being punished for using social media to criticize the government.

SPRING FEVER

IN 2010, a man set himself on fire at a Tunisian market—and set the world on fire, too. He was protesting corruption and government control. As young people began to gather in support, news spread on social media. Tunisia was a country where information couldn't always be freely printed, but suddenly, there was a backchannel.

The rallies grew. And grew.

By January 2011, the president of Tunisia was forced to flee the country. Meanwhile, antigovernment protests had erupted in Egypt. Soon, people were also gathering on the streets of Algeria, Yemen, Libya, Jordan, Bahrain, Morocco, and Syria. The protests would become known as the "Arab Spring."

As the movement swelled, people around the world pointed to the use of cellphones and social media by protesters. They said ordinary students and workers, armed with modern communications, could take down harsh authoritarian governments.

Security forces used their

PRIVACY   PROTECTION

own tech tactics. Egypt and Libya shut down Internet access. Syria was accused of monitoring Facebook and YouTube to target and arrest activists, and apparently enlisted a team of hackers to help. Some news reports suggested officials had bought anti-spam devices from Irish developers. Using those devices, they could screen for keywords about antigovernment protests.

Though protesters managed to oust the old leaders in many countries, not everyone achieved freedom. Tunisia now has a democracy. But in Egypt, the military eventually seized control. Syria spiraled into a brutal civil war. And few citizens in the region have gained free, unmonitored Internet access. Social media and cellphones helped spread the original ideas, but they weren't able to guarantee victory.

All of this points to a familiar conclusion: technology is a tool. And tools can be used in different ways. Cellphones can be used by police as GPS trackers, or by activists for quick communication. Social media can be used to collect surveillance information, or to connect people across borders.

The real questions aren't whether technology helps or hinders surveillance, protects or endangers privacy.

The real questions are these:

1. HOW ARE SOCIETIES GOING TO USE NEW TOOLS?

2. AND WHERE DO WE, AS HUMAN BEINGS, DRAW THE LINE BETWEEN PRIVACY AND PROTECTION?

DRAWING THE LINE

WE UNDERSTAND privacy early in life. As toddlers, we learn not to touch other people's things. We're taught that some parts of our bodies are private. Later, we lock our diaries and draw "keep out" signs for our bedroom doors. We expect strangers to ring doorbells before entering our homes, and we screen telemarketers when they call during dinner.

All of these small actions help to protect our privacy.

Or do they?

These days, there are people, companies, and even products with eyes on our lives. Phone companies track our calls, governments screen our emails, and advertisers parse our social media posts. Stores count our purchases, computers register our fingerprints, and refrigerators mark our milk consumption.

Again and again, social media companies, governments, and advertisers tell us the same things:

→ Surveillance makes us safer.

→ Targeted marketing makes our lives easier.

→ If we're not doing anything wrong, it doesn't matter who's watching.

Meanwhile, privacy advocates offer these warnings:

→ Companies, governments, and police forces use surveillance in ways that could change how we act, protest, or even vote.

→ When we give away our information, we're giving it to every future government and every future company ... data can live forever.

So who's right? Should we embrace trust and openness, and share freely? After all, the level of sharing available on the Internet allows us to connect with people all over the world, learn about other cultures, and exchange information. Or, should we build protective walls to protect ourselves from public shaming, identity theft, and police tracking?

The answers are likely somewhere in the middle. Where, exactly? That's something only the citizens and consumers of the future can decide.

(Hey, wait … that's you!)

FURTHER READING

Brook, Henry. *Spying*. London: Usborne Books, 2014.

Ivester, Matt. *Lol—OMG! What Every Student Needs to Know About Online Reputation Management, Digital Citizenship, and Cyberbullying*. Reno, NV: Serra Knight, 2011.

Jakubiak, David J. *A Smart Kid's Guide to Internet Privacy*. New York: PowerKids Press, 2010.

Linde, Barbara M. *Safe Social Networking*. New York: Gareth Stevens, 2013.

Marzolf, Julie Schwab. *Online Privacy*. New York: Gareth Stevens, 2013.

McHugh, Jeff. *Maintaining a Positive Digital Footprint*. Ann Arbor, Michigan: Cherry Lake Publishing, 2015.

Merino, Noel, ed. *Surveillance*. Farmington Hills, Michigan: Greenhaven Press, 2015.

Roleff, Tamara L. *Privacy*. Farmington Hills, Michigan: Greenhaven Press, 2014.

Teens and Privacy. Detroit, Michigan: Greenhaven Press, 2011.

SELECTED SOURCES

INTRODUCTION

Bilton, Nick. "Social Media Bots Offer Phony Friends and Real Profit." *New York Times,* November 19, 2014.

Thompson, Derek. "Google's CEO: 'The Laws are Written by Lobbyists.'" *The Atlantic,* October 1, 2010.

CHAPTER 1

Bergstein, Brian. "In Online Exams, Big Brother Will Be Watching." *MIT Technology Review,* November 16, 2012. technologyreview.com/news/506346/in-online-exams-big-brother-will-be-watching. Accessed July 17, 2015.

Devlin, Kate. "Nursery Children to Be Fingerprinted." *The Telegraph,* September 23, 2006.

Ema, Arisa, and Yuko Fujigaki. "How Far Can Child Surveillance Go?" *Surveillance and Society,* 2011, 132.

Gicheha, Njenga. "Kenya: Limuru Primary School Puts Up CCTV Cameras." *The Star* (Nairobi), February 19, 2014. allafrica.com/stories/201402191380.html. Accessed November 30, 2015.

Hill, Kashmir. "Court Rejecting Texas Student's Opposition to RFID Tracker Not As Outrageous as It Seems." *Forbes,* January 9, 2013. forbes.com/sites/kash-mirhill/2013/01/09/court-rejecting-texas-students-opposition-to-rfid-tracker-not-as-outrageous-as-it-seems. Accessed July 17, 2015.

–––. "Lower Merion School District and Blake Robbins Reach a Settlement in Spycamgate." *Forbes,* October 11, 2010. forbes.com/sites/kashmirhill/2010/10/11/lower-merion-school-district-and-blake-robbins-reach-a-settlement-in-spycamgate. Accessed July 17, 2015.

Ipsos. "In the US and Canada, Majorities Prefer That Children Attend Schools with Surveillance Cameras over Those Without." ipsos-na.com/news-polls/pressrelease.aspx?id=6157. Accessed June 25, 2015.

Koffler J. "China Uses a Drone to Curb Cheating on College Placement Exams." Time.com, June 12, 2015. Available from: http://time.com/3914087/china-drones-cheating-exams/. Accessed September 21, 2016.

Kravets, David. "School Kicks Out Sophomore in RFID Student-ID Flap." *Wired,* January 18, 2013.

Limuru Model Primary School. "Limuru Model Primary School Background." limuru-model.co.ke/aboutus.html. Accessed November 28, 2015.

Mayer-Schönberger, Viktor, and Kenneth Cukier. *Big Data*. New York: Houghton Mifflin Harcourt Publishing, 2013.

Richer, Jocelyne. "Quebec School Officials No Longer Allowed to Strip Search Students." *Toronto Star,* May 13, 2015.

Rushowy, Kristin. "Toronto School Board Hid Camera in Principal's Office." *Toronto Star,* April 10, 2015.

Shepherd, Jessica. "Someone to Watch Over You." *The Guardian,* August 4, 2009.

Stryker, Alyssa. *Rights Talk.* Vancouver, British Columbia: BC Civil Liberties Association, 2013.

Taylor, Emmeline. "School Surveillance Puts Trust at Risk." *Sydney Morning Herald,* October 8, 2013.

CHaPTer 2

Barron, Carol Margaret. "I Had No Credit to Ring You Back." *Surveillance & Society,* July 1, 2014, 401–13.

Clark, Lynn Shofield. "Digital Media and the Generation Gap." *Information, Communication & Society,* April 1, 2009, 388–407.

Derbyshire, David. "How Children Lost the Right to Roam in Four Generations." *Daily Mail,* June 15, 2007.

Family Safe Media website. familysafemedia.com/iambigbrother_-_parental_control.html. Accessed August 13, 2015.

Gibbs, Samuel. "Hackers Can Hijack Wi-Fi Hello Barbie to Spy on Your Children." *The Guardian,* November 26, 2015.

Ingram, Matt. "Family's Home-Monitoring Camera Hacked; Eerie Voice Speaks." *Globe and Mail,* July 23, 2015.

Kaplan, Caren, et al. "Precision Targets: GPS and the Militarization of Everyday Life." *Canadian Journal of Communication,* 2013, 387–420.

Nelson, Margaret K. *Parenting Out of Control*. New York: New York University Press, 2010.

Pollack, Barbara. "When Does Surveillance Art Cross the Line?" *Art News,* September 9, 2014.

Rooney, Tonya. "Trusting Children." *Surveillance & Society,* July 1, 2014, 344–55.

Shostak, Arthur B., ed. *Moving Along: Far Ahead*. New York: Chelsea House Publishers, 2005.

Teen Safe Driver website. teensafedriver.com. Accessed August 13, 2015.

Yadron, Danny. "VTech Says Data Breach Hit Child Profiles and Adult Accounts." *Wall Street Journal,* December 2, 2015, 1.

CHaPTer 3

"Anti-Social Behaviour Orders—Analysis of the First Six Years." From the website of the government of the United Kingdom. publications.parliament.uk/pa/cm200405/cmselect/cmhaff/80/80we20.htm. Accessed September 11, 2015.

Fonio, Chiara. "Security, Surveillance and Geographical Patterns at the 2010 FIFA World Cup in Johannesburg." *Geographical Journal,* September 1, 2015, 242–48.

Gallagher, Ryan. "Lady Liberty's Watching You." Slate.com. slate.com/articles/technology/future_tense/2013/04/statue_of_liberty_to_get_new_surveillance_tech_but_don_t_mention_face_recognition.html. Accessed September 12, 2015.

Harmel, Karen. "Walt Disney World: The Government's Tomorrowland?" News21, September 1, 2006. news21.com/story/2006/09/01/walt_disney_world_the_governments. Accessed February 12, 2016.

Quinn, Ben. "Anti-Homeless Spikes Are Part of a Wider Phenomenon of 'Hostile Architecture.'" *The Guardian,* June 13, 2014.

Taylor, Adam. "Does an Apple Store Kicking Out Black Teenagers Show Australia Has a Race Problem?" *The Independent* (U.K.), November 12, 2015.

Wolf, Naomi. "The New Totalitarianism of Surveillance Technology." *The Guardian,* December 21, 2012.

CHaPTer 4

Bennett, Colin J., et al., eds. *Transparent Lives*. Edmonton, Alberta: AU Press, 2014.

Bradbury D. "The Kids Are Alright." *Engineering & Technology,* February 2015, 30–33.

"Coquitlam Teen Pleads Guilty in Florida 'Swatting' Case." *Vancouver Sun,* July 9, 2015.

Caesar, Stephen. "Glendale District Says Social Media Monitoring Is for Student Safety." *LA Times,* September 14, 2013.

Christian Elledge, L., et al. "Individual and Contextual Predictors of Cyberbullying." *Journal of Youth & Adolescence,* May 2013, 698–710.

Cyber Civil Rights Initiative. "A message from Our Founder, Dr. Holly Jacobs." cybercivil-rights.org/a_message_from_our_founder_dr_holly_jacobs. Accessed September 22, 2015.

Dickey, Jack. "The Antisocial Network." *Time,* July 7, 2014, 40–45.

Deutsch, Jeremy. "Coquitlam Teenager Sentenced to 16 Months in Jail for 'Swatting.'" *Vancouver Sun,* July 10, 2015.

Get Cybersafe website (Government of Canada). "Think Before You Share." getcybersafe.gc.ca/cnt/rsrcs/pblctns/tnk-bfr-shr-gd/index-en.aspx. Accessed September 24, 2015.

Jarvis, Jeff. *Public Parts*. New York: Simon & Schuster, 2011.

Madden, Mary, et al. "Teens, Social Media, and Privacy." From the website of the Pew Research Center. pewinternet.org/2013/05/21/teens-social-media-and-privacy/. Accessed September 22, 2015.

Marwick, A., and D. Boyd. "Networked Privacy." *New Media & Society,* November 2014, 1051–67.

Messitt M. "Cyberbullying Happens in Code. Break It." *Education Digest,* May 2014, 51–54.

New York Times. "'Kodak Fiends' at Newport." August 18, 1899.

Richards, Neil M., and Daniel J. Solove. "Prosser's Privacy Law." *California Law Review,* December 2010, 1887–1924.

Root, Teri, and Sandra McKay. "Student Awareness of the Use of Social Media Screening by Prospective Employers." *Journal of Education for Business,* May 2014, 202.

Royal Canadian Mounted Police. "Bullying and Cyberbullying." rcmp-grc.gc.ca/cycp-cpcj/bull-inti/index-eng.htm. Accessed February 1, 2016.

Salter, Michael. "Privates in the Online Public." *New Media & Society,* September 7, 2015.

Stolz, Greg, and Tanya Chilcott. "13 Child Suicides in Three Years Prompt Call for Action as Bullying Victims Take Their Own Lives." *Courier Mail* (Australia), May 24, 2013.

Student Press Law Center. "Bell v. Itawamba County School Board." splc.org article/2014/08/bell-v-itawamba-county-school-board. Accessed December 1, 2015.

Vickery, J. R. "'I Don't Have Anything to Hide, But...'" *Information, Communication & Society,* March 2015, 281–94.

Williams, Mary Elizabeth. "Curt Schilling Goes After the Trolls Who Went After His Daughter." *Salon,* March 3, 2015. salon.com/2015/03/03/curt_schilling_goes_after_the_trolls_who_went_after_his_daughter/. Accessed September 22, 2015.

CHAPTER 5

Dale, Brady. "Internet-Connected Egg Holders Win Connected Fridge Hackathon." *Observer,* June 22, 2015. observer.com/2015/06/chillhub-hackathon-internet-refrigerator-makerbot-ge-firstbuild/. Accessed October 9, 2015.

Duhigg, Charles. "How Companies Learn Your Secrets." *New York Times Magazine,* February 16, 2012.

Grossman, L. "What's This All About?" *Time,* July 6, 2015, 41–43.

IBM. "The Four V's of Big Data." ibmbigdatahub.com/infographic/four-vs-big-data. Accessed May 22, 2015.

Kosinski, M., D. Stillwell, and T. Graepel. "Private Traits and Attributes Are Predictable from Digital Records of Human Behavior." *Proceedings of the National Academy of Sciences of the United States of America,* 2013 (5): 802–5.

Newe, Gary. "Delivering the Internet of Things." *Network Security,* March 2015, 18–20.

Popa, M., et al. "Analysis of Shopping Behavior Based on Surveillance System." Systems, Man, and Cybernetics (SMC), 2010 IEEE International Conference, October 10–13, 2010 (2): 512–19. ieee.org/conferences_events/conferences/conferencedetails/index.html?Conf_ID=16229.

CHAPTER 6

Bennett, Colin J., et al., eds. *Transparent Lives.* Edmonton, Alberta: AU Press, 2014.

Carter, Mike. "FBI Confirms It Used Fake News Story, Denies Bogus Times Web Link." *Seattle Times,* October 28, 2014. seattletimes.com/seattle-news/fbi-confirms-it-used-fake-story-denies-bogus-times-web-link/. Accessed November 5, 2015.

Cristillo, Dr. Louis. "Religiosity, Education, and Civic Belonging." *Teachers College Columbia University,* April 20, 2008, 12.

The Economist. "The Most Persecuted People on Earth?" June 13, 2015, 37–40.

Ganascia, J. "The Generalized Sousveillance Society." *Social Science Information,* September 2010, 489–507.

Gatehouse, Jonathon. "You Are Exposed." *Maclean's,* November 21, 2005, 26–29.

Greenwald, Glenn. *No Place to Hide.* New York: Metropolitan Books, 2014.

Grewal, San, et al. "End of the Road for Random Street Checks." *Toronto Star,* October 23, 2015, A1.

Hattenstone, Simon. "Mark Kennedy." *The Guardian,* March 26, 2011. theguardian.com/environment/2011/mar/26/mark-kennedy-undercover-cop-environmental-activist. Accessed November 5, 2015.

IRIN. "Bangladesh: New ID Card Policies Could Hit Rohingya Asylum-Seekers." irinnews.org/report/92302/bangladesh-new-id-card-policy-could-hit-rohingya-asylum-seekers. Accessed December 1, 2015.

Journal of Transportation. "Most Americans Willing to Sacrifice Some Privacy to Enhance Safe Air Travel, According to Latest Unisys Security Index." May 1, 2010, 95.

Liu, J. "Mobile Communication, Popular Protests and Citizenship in China." *Modern Asian Studies,* May 2013, 995–1018.

Lubbers, Eveline. "Undercover Research." *Surveillance & Society,* 2015, 338–53.

Nihal, Mariam. "Uproar Over E-tracking System for Saudi Women Travelers." *Saudi Gazette,* November 29, 2012.

Potoglou, Dimitris, et al. "Quantifying Individuals' Trade-Offs Between Privacy, Liberty and Security: The Case of Rail Travel in UK." *Transportation Research Part A, Policy and Practice,* 2010, 169–81.

Sinha, G. Alex. "NSA Surveillance Since 9/11 and the Human Right to Privacy." *Loyola Law Review,* December 2013, 861.

Soldatov, Andrei. "Russia's Surveillance State." *World Policy Journal,* September 1, 2013, 23.

Ullah, Akm Ahsan. "Rohingya Refugees to Bangladesh." *Journal of Immigrant & Refugee Studies,* April 1, 2011, 139–61.

Wike, Richard. "Ratings of Muslims Rise in France After Charlie Hebdo, Just As in U.S. after 9/11." From the website of the Pew Research Center. pewresearch.org/fact-tank/2015/06/03/ratings-of-muslims-in-france-and-us/. Accessed December 1, 2015.

Zheng, Haiping. "Regulating the Internet: China's Law and Practice." *Beijing Law Review,* 2013, 37–41.

INDEX

advertising 4, 93, 122–23.
    See also marketing
air travel 114
alarm companies 34
Algeria 120
American Family
        Insurance 35
Amnesia 65
Amnesty International 117
Angola 62
Anonymous 12
anxiety 29
Apple 54, 95
Arab Spring 120
Arctic 32
Argentina 62
Ashton, Kevin 99
Asia 13
Ask.fm 69, 70
Australia 54, 66, 81
Australian Human Rights
        Commission 66
autism 36

baby monitors 29–31, 34
Bahrain 120
Bangladesh 105
Barbie 34
Belgium 66, 94, 107
Bell, Taylor 78–79
Bentham, Jeremy 7
biometrics 20–21, 22, 56
Bird, William 27
bomb threats 70, 112. *See
        also* terrorism
Boston Marathon
        bombing 45–46
Boston Red Sox 74
Brandeis, Louis 60, 81
Brazil 37
Breathalyzer test 22
Britain 14, 21, 27–29, 49,
        53, 81, 107,
        110–11, 114
    surveillance cameras
        in 14, 44

bullying 14
cameras 44
    Kodak 61
    See also cellphones,
        surveillance
        cameras
Canada 53, 65, 70, 103,
        104, 107, 112
Canadian Civil Liberties
        Association 22
carding 109–110
catopticon 113
cellphones 2, 23, 38,
        42–43, 51, 64, 73
    as cameras 45, 113
    as protest tools 119,
        120–21
    as tracking devices
        33–34, 36, 42–43,
        90, 95, 96, 103–4,
        115
censorship 79, 117
Charlie Hebdo 114
cheating 17
China 16–17, 66, 118–19
civil liberties 24
Cleland, Jessica 66
Clementi, Tyler 66
Copenhagen 14
corporations 4, 83–88,
        101, 122–23
credit cards 77, 78, 86
crime 4, 8, 29, 57, 77–78,
        107, 108–9.
        See also
        Boston Marathon
        bombing,
        doxxing, hacking,
        kidnapping,
        swatting
Crisis Text Line 117
Cyber Civil Rights
        Initiative 75
cyberbulling 65–66
cybersecurity 35

data 4, 63, 64, 75, 85, 86,
        88–90, 93–96,
        100–101, 107, 108,
        123
    health 116–17
    mining 88
depression 29, 69, 117
digital tattoo 63, 82
Disneyland 70
DNA 20, 108
doxxing 73–74
drones 17, 61, 97
drugs 19, 38–39

Eastman, George 61
Egypt 120–21
Elf on the Shelf 34
Ema, Arisa 25–26
email 2, 38, 39, 51, 64, 73,
        76, 103–4, 106,
        108
environmental activists
        47, 110–11
equiveillance 113
Europe 13, 36, 75

Facebook 2, 56, 59, 63, 65,
        78, 81, 91–92,
        121, 122
facial recognition
        technology 48, 54,
        56, 90, 97
Federal Bureau of
        Investigation (FBI)
        45–46, 75, 112
Felsen, Ron 22
FIFA World Cup 48
fingerprints 20–21, 83,
        122
    false 17
Finland 67
First Nations 112
Fitbit 95–96
fitness 95–96
Fort Meade High School
        70

Foster, Martha and Matthew 39
France 103, 114–15
Fujigaki, Yuko 25–26

Gallagher, Ryan 54–55
Ganascia, Jean-Gabriel 113
Germany 66, 103
Global Positioning System (GPS) 32–33, 36–37, 38, 39, 115, 121
Google 5, 75, 95
government surveillance 103–21, 122–23

hacking 20, 21, 31, 35, 73, 121. *See also* Anonymous, doxxing
harassment 64–65, 74, 75 by police 109–10, *See also* carding, cyberbulling, doxxing
Hattersley, Jack 27–29
Hello Kitty 91
Hernandez, Andrea 11–13
Homyk, Matthew 69
Hong Kong 21, 44, 104

IBM 88
identity theft 77–78
India 66
Instagram 63
Internet of Things 98–99
Internet providers 2
Ipsos Public Affairs 14
Ireland 42–43, 66, 111
iris scans 20–21
Italy 65, 66
Itawamba Agricultural High School 78–79

Jacobs, Holly 75

Japan 9, 25–26, 51, 66
Jawbone UP 95-96
John Jay High 11–13, 14
Jones, Sally 114
Jordan 120

Kennedy, Mark 110–11
Kenya 15
keytrackers 38
kidnapping 29, 36–37
Kodak 61, 63

Latvia 70
libraries 11, 21
Libya 120–21
Limuru Model Primary School 15
Louyang, China 17
loyalty cards 85, 86, 88

Maclean's 107
macroscope 96
Maker Faire 100
Malaysia 105
malls 51–52
marketing 84–85, 86, 93, 95, 101
McDonald's 5
Mexico 36–37
Minecraft 72
Morocco 120
Mosquito devices 49
Mount Everest 32
Myanmar 105
MySpace 112

nanny cams 30
National College Entrance Exam 16–17
National Security Agency (NSA) 103, 107
Natural England 27
"Neighbors, The" 39
Netflix 88
New York City 39
New York Times 61

New York Times Magazine 84
New Zealand 103
Nineteen Eighty-Four 104

obfuscation 94
online shopping 8, 83, 88
Orwell, George 104

panopticon 7, 23, 113
parents 14, 25–26, 29–31, 27–43
passports 11
passwords 72, 82
PEN International 117
Pennsylvania 19
pets 11, 32
Pew Research Center 64
phishing 76–78
Pole, Andrew 84–85
police 4, 45–46, 57, 75, 94, 108–10, 118–19, 121, 123 and carding 109–10 and cyberbullying 67 and swatting 70
political parties 93
Prabhu, Trisha 68
predictive policing 108–9
preschools 13, 21
privacy agreements 96
privacy laws 62
Prosser, William 62
pseudonyms 81
public health 116–17

racial profiling 109–10
radio frequency identification (RFID) 9–11, 22, 23, 25–26, 37, 117
radio transmitters 17
Rebaudengo, Simone 98
religious freedom 11–13
right to be forgotten 75
Robbins, Blake 19–20

INDEX

Rohingya 105
Roosevelt, President
      Theodore 61
Russia 104, 106
Rwanda 107

Saudi Arabia 53, 115
Schilling, Curt 74–75
Schmidt, Eric 5
schools 9–26
      alarms 15
      cameras 12, 13, 14, 15,
            22–24
      online courses 18–19
      social media moni-
            toring 79
      student ID cards
            11–13
      video streaming 13
      security cameras. See
      surveillance cameras
selfies 6
Selvaggio, Leo 51
shopping 47, 83–90.
            See also malls,
            online shopping
Shufen, Li 118–19
Shutterfly 56
Singapore 97
skateboarding 49
smartphones. See
            cellphones
Snapchat 63, 81
Snowden, Edward 104,
      106
social contagion 92
social media 5, 8, 59–82,
      93, 103, 119,
      120–21, 123. See
      also Ask.fm,
      Facebook,
      Instagram,
      Shutterfly,
      Snapchat, Tumblr,
      Twitter, YouTube

sousveillance 113
South Africa 49
South Korea 57, 68
Spain 66
Statue of Liberty 54–55
Stone, Mark 110–11
suicide 16, 65–66, 69, 118
surgical masks 51
surveillance cameras 2,
      44, 45–46, 47–48,
      57–58, 89, 108
      in cars 34
      in malls 52
      in parks 54–55
      in public places 49
      in schools 2, 12, 13, 14,
            15, 22–24
surveillance creep 108
Svenson, Arne 39
Sweden 66
Syria 120–21

Target 84–85
TEDx 68
Teen Safe Driver program
      35
television 27
terrorism 4, 45–46, 94,
      107, 114–15
texting 6, 43, 68, 115,
      116–17, 118–19
      while driving 36
Thomas, George 27–29,
      43
thoughtcrime 104
Todd, Amanda 65
toys 34–35
traffic 47
trilateration 32
Trump, Donald 73
trust 38–39, 41–42
Tsarnaev, Dzhokhar and
      Tamerlan 46
Tumblr 63, 81
Tunisia 114, 120–121

Turkey 66
Twitter 2, 63, 66

UNICEF 105
United States 11–13, 14,
      66, 68, 70, 78–79,
      81, 93, 100, 103,
      104, 108, 109–10,
      111–12, 114, 116

University of Cambridge
      91
U.S. National Park System
      54–55, 61
vandalism 14
Venezuela 62
video games 27
video streaming 13, 34
Voice, The 6
VTech 35

Walmart 11
Warren, Samuel 60, 81
webcams 6, 18–20, 101
White House 68
World Health
            Organization 9
World Trade Center 114
World War II 11

Yemen 120
YouTube 63, 65, 78, 113,
      121

Zimbabwe 62

ABOUT THE AUTHOR & ILLUSTRATOR

Since researching *Eyes and Spies,* TANYA LLOYD KYI has covered her webcams with sticky notes, changed all of her passwords, and refrained from singing karaoke with her hairbrush as a microphone (just in case anyone's watching). That's left her plenty of time to write. She's the author of more than 20 books for children and young adults, including *Extreme Battlefields, DNA Detective,* and *When the Worst Happens.* She lives in Vancouver, B.C.

BELLE WUTHRICH is a freelance illustrator and designer in Vancouver, BC. She has a Bachelor in Communication Design from Emily Carr University of Art + Design. She works from her eye-in-the-sky panopticon-like building with her vigilant cat minions, Louie and Winston. The tiny people they observe below never suspect that they may become the inspiration for her next illustration. *Eyes & Spies* is the third book that she has illustrated for Annick Press ... but keep that under your hat!

LOOK FOR THESE OTHER GREAT
BOOKS FROM ANNICK PRESS

Made You Look: How Advertising Works and Why You Should Know

Revised Edition
by Shari Graydon
illustrated by Michelle Lamoreaux

PAPERBACK $16.95 | HARDCOVER $26.95

* Best Books for Kids & Teens, Canadian Children's Book Centre

"The thoughtful and balanced presentation, clear explanations and entertaining real-life examples are a solid starting point for getting children—and adults—to think critically about the way that products are advertised." —*The Guardian*

"Data-filled and slightly tongue-in-cheek ... informs young consumers." —*Curriculum Connections*, Editor's Choice

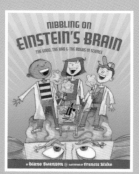

Nibbling on Einstein's Brain: The Good, the Bad, and the Bogus in Science

Revised Edition
By Diane Swanson
Illustrated by Francis Blake

PAPERBACK $12.95 | HARDCOVER $24.95

Winner of numerous awards and accolades, including:
* Booklist's Top 10 Sci-Tech Books for Youth, 2002
* VOYA's Non-Fiction Honor List, 2002
* White Raven Collection, International Youth Library, Munich, 2002
* Eisenhower Collection of Math and Science Books , 2002
* Best Books, Canadian Children's Book Centre, 2010

Research Ate My Brain: The Panic-Proof Guide to Surviving Homework

by Toronto Public Library
illustrated by Martha Newbigging

PAPERBACK $9.95 / $8.95 US | HARDCOVER $19.95

* Our Choice List, Canadian Children's Book Centre
* Public Library Service Award nomination

"... will be of interest to researchers, or just information gatherers, of all ages and stages." —*The Globe and Mail*

"It's all good, solid information ... teens needing research help would seek out this concise, accurate guide and refer to it often." —*Quill & Quire*